# IT'S TIME TO GROW
### *Kick-starting a church into growth*

# IT'S
# TIME TO
# GROW

*Kick-starting a church into growth*

## Colin Dye

Gazelle Books

Harpenden, Herts AL5 4SE
ENGLAND

First published 1997
by Gazelle Books, Station Road, Harpenden, Herts, AL5 4SE
England, UK

ISBN 1 899746 10 2

Biblical quotations are from the *New King James Version*
© Thomas Nelson Inc., 1982

**British Library Cataloguing in Publication Data.**
A record for this book is available from the British Library.

Designed and Produced in England for
GAZELLE BOOKS
by Nuprint Ltd, Station Road, Harpenden, Herts AL5 4SE.

# Dedication

*For the people of Kensington Temple, the congregations of the London City Church Network, and all those who are deeply committed to the growth of the Church of Jesus Christ in the world today*

# CONTENTS

Foreword                                      9

Introduction                                 11

1.  Getting to grips with the church         13

2.  God wants your church to grow            41

3.  Getting the vision right                 72

4.  Getting the details right                92

5.  Putting people first                    117

6.  Creative evangelism                     144

# Foreword

Church planting and church growth are two subjects which have fascinated me ever since I graduated from Theological College.

In those days, there was very little written on these two subjects. No conferences were organised to help ministers who were burdened to plant and grow churches. Successful pastors of large churches did not spend time helpfully advising younger pastors. Any literature on the topics was written by theorists rather than by practitioners.

Over the years, I have come to believe that – just as genes in the human body make it impossible for us not to grow – so the Holy Spirit has planted genes in the church which make it impossible for the church not to grow.

I see that the early church grew in leaps and bounds. The only small church then was a 'new' church – but it did not stay small long as God soon added people to it.

Colin Dye is not just a theorist about planting and growing churches. I do not know of any other church in Europe which has planted as many churches as Kensington Temple. Through Colin's leadership, over one hundred new churches have been 'birthed'.

Colin has devised teaching programmes to assist the

leadership in growing new churches. He has established a Bible School to train the necessary pastors. He is a 'risk-taker' and foresees leadership potential in men and women who would not otherwise have an opportunity to lead and develop their embryonic leadership skills.

In this book, Colin shares his heart, his wisdom and his experience in this vital branch of God's work. Here is great teaching, sound advice and prime examples of 'how it works in practice'.

I commend this book to you, and pray that it will challenge many of God's servants to 'grow the church' under their care.

*Rev. Wynne Lewis*
*General Superintendent*
*Elim Pentecostal Churches*

# Introduction

Although I do not consider myself to be an expert on church growth, the churches I lead have experienced growth. This has meant that, in the last few years, I have faced the challenge of helping a growing church to continue in growth.

Rather than focusing on trying to develop an American-style 'mega-church' consisting of one huge congregation, we set ourselves the goal – which we are beginning to achieve – of planting one new church or congregation every week. This has demanded that we concentrate our physical and spiritual energies on making smaller churches grow.

Some of these new churches have now grown to over 500 people, but our average congregation contains around 50 people. My aim in writing this book is simply to help leaders of smaller churches benefit from our experience and breakthrough into new and increasing levels of growth.

I have tried to do this essentially by identifying and examining the scriptural principles that we have followed at Kensington Temple and within the London City Church Network. However, I have also included many practical

11

ideas which seem to be facilitating continued growth in our smaller congregations, and several testimonies from leaders of our new churches. There are also several questions at the end of each chapter which have been included to help you understand and apply the material in your own situation. Please don't ignore them! You should gain considerable benefit from taking time to answer the questions and think through your response to the issues they raise.

Any study of church growth must surely be set in the context of the present world-wide increase in effective evangelism. It seems to me that God is moving faster, and with greater intensity, in these days than ever before.

Some reports claim that 70% of all the evangelism which has ever taken place has occurred in this century. Furthermore, it is suggested that 70% of this has happened since 1945, and that 70% of this has taken place in the last four years.

These figures highlight the way that the Spirit's outpouring accelerated during the twentieth century. This led some people to look towards the year 2,000 with great expectancy. But God is not tied to artificial Western calendar systems, and we do not know when Jesus will return or what lies before us.

However, we do know that we have only this generation to reach this generation. Many are relying on modern technology to intensify contemporary evangelism. But I believe that our lost generation will best be reached with the gospel through a multitude of small, growing, multiplying, interdependent congregations.

We should try to remain focused on the urgency of the task of reaching our generation while we examine those factors which seem to help small churches to grow.

# ONE

# Getting to grips with the church

Whenever our enthusiasm has been dampened by the day to day details of church life – or we sense that our congregation's spiritual life is not what it should be – we need to get to grips with a vision of the church which will lift us out of our depression.

We need to start dwelling on the glorious destiny that God has for his church. We must see ourselves as we truly are – tightly held in the stream of God's eternal plan. We must remember that God is calling to himself one people, drawn from every nation, whose destination is heaven. And we are part of this.

In some amazing way that we neither understand nor appreciate, we are joined through the cross to countless millions of believers in every country and continent right across the world. And we are united with vast multitudes of brothers and sisters who are gathered round the throne of the lamb of God, with those believers who are already dwelling in his glory in his heavenly kingdom.

### *The final destiny*

We understand that God's church will be redeemed and liberated by the blood of Christ. We value the scriptures' promise that the church will be forgiven and cleansed, made useful and effective, given a glorious eternal inheritance and built into a habitation of God in the Spirit. We are certain that the church is Christ's body, that it is the fullness of him who fills all in all. And we know that we are part of this.

Our tiny local congregations – with all their earthly imperfections and human inadequacies – are inexorably being drawn by God towards a wonderful final destiny.

We *will* come to the unity of the faith. We *will* reach the knowledge of the Son of God. We *will* form the perfect Man. We *will* be fully mature with the fullness of Christ. We *will* be filled with the utter fullness of God. We *will* be united with all things in heaven and on earth under one head, even Jesus Christ.

If we can grip hold of this accurate, scriptural vision of the church, we will find that it keeps us going when we are brought low by the routine of Sunday by Sunday preaching, by the seemingly endless round of counselling and committee meetings, by the dissensions and difficulties of daily church life.

Whether we realise it or not, we are working towards the fulfilment of this vision whenever we plan and pray and strategise. We bring the vision one step closer to completion every time we mobilise our members for the work of Christ, every time we worship God in spirit and truth, every time we communicate the good news effectively.

Very soon, much sooner than we think, we will find ourselves in the presence of Jesus. Even if he delays in his coming, our life span on earth will be over in a flash. But as we labour on earth with and for Jesus, we are investing in considerable heavenly treasure.

This does not mean that we are escaping from the problems and concerns of earth, for the church is built on the earth and is composed of people who have consider-able needs and problems.

Instead, God calls his followers to be involved with the concerns of earth. We are meant to influence our world for Christ, to see God's kingdom established in the lives of people around us, to make a difference to our com-munities by living as salt and light.

We can effectively fulfil this calling only from within the church, for it is against the church that the gates of hell cannot prevail. This is why I believe we must be involved in the work of growing and multiplying churches. Quite simply, this is a task of enormous eternal significance.

## BACK TO BASIC BIBLICAL PRINCIPLES

When I study the New Testament, I see several basic bib-lical principles which govern us as the church. I do not think that there is a rigid pattern which must be applied in every small detail. Instead there are examples and gen-eral principles that should be followed by any expression of the church which sincerely desires to grow.

I believe that New Testament principles are relevant to today, and that we can expect to experience growth when we follow them. Where there is no growth, it may just be that one of these elementary principles is somehow being violated.

I think it is vital that we have an accurate understand-ing of the basic biblical ideas about the church. I hope that I will never stop increasing my appreciation of the biblical church, for there is so much in scripture that I have yet to grasp. If we are serious about the church, we will keep on reading and re-reading the word of God – especially in times of renewal.

I believe that God is restoring the glory to the church that it had in its first days. But I also believe that he is going to transcend that glory and surpass it with the greater glory of the end-time church. If I am right, this means that we should both be looking backwards to the

New Testament and also looking forward to what lies ahead.

## Ekklesia

The Bible uses two great words to describe the church. *Ekklesia* is the Greek word which is most commonly used. It is derived from the two words *ek*, out of, and *klesis*, a calling: it literally means 'called out'.

But the everyday use of *ekklesia* in New Testament times went much further than describing just a 'calling out'. *Ekklesia* was used by Greeks to identify the group of citizens who gathered to discuss important state affairs. They were 'the assembly'. A herald would go through the city announcing the gathering, and those who were summoned would gather together on state business.

This means that, whenever a Christian evangelist proclaims, the result is the assembly or the church. This highlights the crucial connection between evangelism and church growth.

Although every person must hear the gospel for themselves, and believe in Jesus individually, we do not have an individualistic faith. When the calling from Christ is heard, we find that we are part of his *ekklesia* – his assembly or gathering.

The word 'church' has many unhelpful associations today. If we look it up in a dictionary, the first meaning we read is 'a place for public Christian worship'; but this is not a biblical interpretation of *ekklesia*. Unfortunately, although most believers know that the church is not the building, they still focus their activities around their building.

A worse contemporary misunderstanding is the confusion of church with meetings. We often hear people ask, 'Are you going to church on Sunday?' Yet what they really mean is, 'Are you going to the meeting?' *Ekklesia* does mean a gathering; but meetings are merely one expression of the gathering, not its essential substance.

*Ekklesia* is fundamentally a matter of relationship. It is the word for our cross-forged relationships both with

Jesus Christ and with all other believers – those who are
alive on earth and those who are already worshipping
him in heaven.

Once it has begun, this relationship exists for twenty
four hours a day, seven days a week, on into and
throughout eternity. It is unbiblical to think that we
assemble in buildings or meetings to 'be' or 'do' church –
and that we then leave church until the next coming
together. Yet this approach is regularly practised in many
churches.

We must change our thinking on this point. We are not
*ekklesia* because we come together; we come together
because we are *ekklesia*. There is a huge difference
between the two ideas, and the way we think about this
will have major implications for our approach to church
growth.

If our thinking about church – our 'ecclesiology' – is
building or meeting centred, our strategies and aims for
growing a church will reflect this. We will assume that bigger and better buildings, or carefully manicured and culturally meaningful meetings are the most important key to
growth.

Obviously I agree that meeting together is one of the
highest expressions of *ekklesia*. Yet surely the purpose of
our gathering together in meetings and buildings is to
encourage each other to go out and be the church in the
community, to be the church in our homes, to be the
church at our place of work – to be *ekklesia* all day long.

The book of Acts shows us that the first Christians continually expressed *ekklesia*. They met in the temple and
they met in each other's homes. They encouraged one
another. They performed good deeds and charitable acts.
They grasped every opportunity to witness and to live as
the body of Christ in their community.

## Koinonia

The Greek word *koinonia* is the second great word that
the New Testament uses to describe the church. *Koinonia*

is derived from *koinos*, which means 'common', and is usually translated as 'fellowship'.

Like *ekklesia*, *koinonia* is a relationship word. It means 'sharing together with a clear common purpose', and refers to the fellowship that we have – by the cross and by the Spirit – with God and each other. *Koinonia* shows that we stand together in a relationship in which we participate together in Christ.

As Christians, we hold Christ in common. We share him, we share in him, and we share together in all the things of God. This is what the New Testament means by 'the fellowship' or 'the communion' of saints.

Some believers consider fellowship, *koinonia*, to be one of the church's activities – what happens at the end of the meetings. But fellowship encircles everything that we have, are and do as believers. Quite simply, it is an alternative word for church.

All genuine fellowship is founded in Christ. All that we share together as Christians, we share in Jesus. We exist together in him, and have him in common. And all true fellowship is accomplished by the Holy Spirit – who is himself the Spirit of fellowship. Through the Spirit, we participate in the Son; and, through the Spirit, we are in relationship with all other believers who live in him.

This is something that I particularly notice when I am travelling. When I arrive in a remote part of the world, I am usually greeted by people who have never met me before. Yet there is an immediate bond between us because we recognise that we have Jesus in common.

Fellowship is not something we share with each other merely by performing certain external actions. Jesus is with us through his Spirit. We share him in each other. We recognise him in our brothers and sisters and sense a oneness that we can never feel with those who are not yet part of the faith.

Acts 2:42 describes how the first converts devoted themselves to *koinonia*. This does not mean the informal aspects of church life – the bits before and after meetings. *Koinonia* includes *everything* that we are called to do together as Christians. This is why Acts 2:42 identifies the church as *the* fellowship. The new disciples were not devoted to drinking coffee and discussing news, but to sharing together in a dynamic and purposeful relationship.

## *The universal church*

The New Testament does not use *ekklesia* and *koinonia* to describe the church in only one way. Instead, it uses them to present the church in three different, yet complementary, ways. Through these words, we are introduced to the concepts of the universal church, local churches, and household churches.

Each of these three ways of expressing *ekklesia* and *koinonia* is valid on its own. However, a complete picture of the church can be seen only by grasping and appreciating all three expressions. Again, the way that we think about these concepts will critically effect our understanding of, and our approach to, church growth.

The universal church is the body of Christ. It consists of all genuine Christians everywhere – both on earth and in heaven. It is invisible and has no expression of its own. We cannot meet together until Christ returns. We cannot share communion together this side of eternity. There may be some multi-national events when different international parts of Christ's body on earth can recognise each other. But the first joint-convention of the church's earthly and heavenly divisions is still rather a long way off!

This means that no church gathering on earth can rightly be considered to be either the universal church or the body of Christ. Every gathering of the church is just a small expression of the universal church, and even the largest congregation is only a tiny part of the body of Christ. The one universal church, the single body of Christ, reveals itself on earth through *all* local and *all* household churches.

## *Local churches*

I think that, today, we should hesitate to use the phrase 'local church', because New Testament 'local churches' were far, far away from what we now consider 'local churches' to be.

In the New Testament, a local church consisted of *all* the believers in a locality – like a town, a city or a rural area. For example, when Paul wrote to the church in Corinth, it was not to a small community assembly which was tucked away in a suburban side-street serving a tiny area. He wrote to a vast metropolitan church which had many congregations and Christian meetings all over the city. The local church in Corinth was the church throughout the city.

New Testament local churches were strong visible expressions of the body of Christ in a recognisable geographical area. These churches were usually broken down into smaller expressions of *ekklesia* – which each functioned as fully fledged churches.

What we call 'local churches' today are nearly always much smaller units of *ekklesia* than the church of an urban or rural region. Sadly, they often function independently of other churches in the same locality. This was not so in the New Testament, when all the churches in a region joined and co-operated together as the church in that locality.

## Household churches

Households were much larger in New Testament times and were seen as communities in their own right, so churches developed naturally within these social structures. There were no formal church buildings in those days, so large homes were the obvious place for believers to meet. I think that we can helpfully call these expressions of *ekklesia* 'community churches'.

New Testament household or community churches were fully functioning churches which expressed *ekklesia* and *koinonia*, had clear leadership, and appear to have done everything that churches should do. They were not independent units, but interdependent parts of the local church. I suspect it is likely that the local church leadership was drawn from among the household church leaders.

In the New Testament, believers were identified as part of the local church – the church in Ephesus, Corinth and so on. But some of these churches were enormous and would themselves have consisted of large numbers of communities or households. So today's archetypal modern congregation is much closer to a household church than to the other biblical expressions of *ekklesia*.

Community or household churches have been overlooked in many recent studies of the church. This has meant that some leaders have attempted to apply the principles and examples of New Testament local churches to contemporary local churches.

For example, although 1 Corinthians was written to the church in Corinth (to a networked interdependent group of household churches) its teaching is usually applied today to individual congregations – to independent community churches. This means that a passage like 1 Corinthians 11:18 is used by pastors to deal with divisions within their congregation rather than to heal disunity between congregations. And passages like 1 Corinthians 12:1-30 are applied congregationally rather than corporately.

Of course, every passage about the universal or local church is relevant to community churches. But the difference between the applications I have mentioned is considerable, and a consequence of our current Western infatuation with individualism.

The misunderstanding about the nature of local churches has led some to believe that a modern congregation must be numerically large before it can function biblically. Leaders who try to establish a modern community church on the first century pattern for a local church usually develop an independent, self-contained congregation which has a large number of members and one strong leader.

Such churches depend on unusually gifted leadership, expensive and glamorous buildings – and grow only by addition. I call this 'top down' growth.

Community churches, however, are essentially small and *inter*dependent. They are flexible about their build-

ings. They are led by ordinary people. They depend on
training and relationships. And their growth is 'bottom
up'. They grow in a constant cycle of addition and division which results in the multiplication of smaller
churches.

Because they are interdependent, they sometimes meet
together to express their dynamic relationships in celebration. These occasional large celebrations may have the
appearance of a single, independent congregation at worship, but the weekly life and leadership structure of a network of such churches is entirely different.

For me, passages like Romans 16:10-11; 1 Corinthians
16:19; Colossians 4:15 and Philemon 1:1 suggest that the
Holy Spirit is drawing our attention to modern communities. It seems to me that it is God's goal to have an expression of *ekklesia* in every community and that our thinking
about church – and especially church growth – should
focus upon these smaller community churches.

The community for us may be a village, a small town,
a section of a city suburb, even a street, an ethnic or special interest group. As co-workers with Christ, we must
seek to express *ekklesia* and *koinonia* in every single
*community*. However we must also seek to express the
church in every *locality* – across cities, towns, rural
regions and, if possible, at a national level.

Denominational structures can help us develop this
identity nationally. They can be a powerful expression of
*ekklesia* and *koinonia*, but only when they are not exclusive. We must always share together across other streams,
traditions and denominations.

As leaders, we must help our people to discover the joy
of *ekklesia* at every level of church life – and encourage
them to be involved with the church at both their local
*and* at their community level.

But does this concept of three complementary expressions of *ekklesia* have any practical application for church
growth? I believe that it does, because every individual
member needs to appreciate their identity as a member of
the one body of Christ – of the universal church.

As leaders, we rob them of this position when we do not encourage them to express the church according to biblical principles. It is as we work in our communities that we reach people for Jesus, but it is as we join together across the locality that we discover our identity in the church.

When we join together as a genuine biblical local church we are enabled to hear what the Spirit is saying to the churches. Many changes can happen at a community church level when people are in touch with developments across the local church. The pastors find less opposition to any changes that God wants to bring. The people know that this is what God is saying and doing among other believers and churches. They know that what is being introduced is a genuine move of God's Spirit across an area or nation.

## Leadership

One of the most basic biblical principles about the church is that there must be clearly defined leadership. I do not think that it necessarily matters what title leaders are given, or what system of church government is followed; the most basic principle is simply that leaders are called to lead.

Leaders are not called to follow the congregation, or merely to do what the congregation tells them to do. Instead, leaders are called to lead the congregation into the will of God.

Of course, this requires consensus through discussion, prayer, co-operation and agreement. But leaders must lead.

Personally, I believe in a corporate style of leadership – even in the smallest churches – but any team of leaders must have someone who, under Christ, is recognised as the leader.

Although ships are led by a team of officers who each have specific responsibilities, each ship must have a captain. Any ship without a captain is directionless and a danger to other shipping in the area. It is the same in the church.

## Membership

Related to this is the principle that there must be clearly defined members in the church. Just as a captain and officers cannot sail a ship without a crew, so leaders need members to make the church function. Something is not right in a church if the leader is leading on his or her own, and nobody is following them.

The membership consists of those people who are called by the Spirit into relationship with each other and the leaders in a particular expression of the church.

Again, I do not think it matters which system of membership is followed, nor what members are called. There simply needs to be some way of recognising the people who are committed to each other and the leaders within each expression of the church.

In Ephesians 4, Paul likens this sort of relationship to the human body. Although he is referring specifically to the universal church rather then to local or community churches, the wider application has some validity.

Every expression of the church should be bound together by something like the joints, ligaments and sinews which bind the human body together. These are not institutional rules, membership lists or legal constitutions. Real membership exists by the Spirit because the body of Christ is a living, growing, changing, maturing organism.

This means that we must teach people to acknowledge the relationships that the Spirit is seeking to develop in and between churches. And, as leaders, we must make time to allow the Spirit to help us develop them.

There is genuine strength and security when people are in a spiritual relationship in a church. Even when they disagree with some of the things that are happening, or other members insult or offend them, they will hold fast to the fellowship. Why? Because they know God has put them in a relationship with that part of the one body.

### Stewardship

It is fundamental to our thinking about the church to recognise that it is the unique body of Christ and – as such – has a vital task. The church does not exist for the comfort or entertainment of its members. We are not here to provide a building where people can sing hymns on a Sunday or gossip during the week. Instead, God has commissioned his church – his body – to be stewards of the gospel: to pass on the good news about Jesus Christ.

The universal church has a task, a calling, a critical function on earth. It is the body of Christ. We act as his hands and feet and mouth in our particular community. We should be saying and doing only what he is saying and doing. Members of growing churches know that, as the church, they should proclaim and demonstrate the crucified, risen Lord Jesus.

As a church serves its community, so Christ is glorified. It might not be popular as it evangelises or stands for truth and righteousness, but these are essential tasks for it to carry out. I have found that a church starts to fulfil its role on earth once it begins to understand it.

I think that there is a simple three-fold mission for every expression of the church. We are called to make disciples, to mature disciples and to mobilise disciples. When any part of the church – with the Spirit's strength and guidance – makes these three tasks its highest priority, it will find that it has already started to become a growing church.

### Partnership

My final basic principle of the church is that every part exists in partnership. Congregations are not isolated units but part of a much larger whole. Together, all churches are members of the one body of Christ. It is simply not right to think or to act as if our particular congregation, tradition or group is all that there is to the church.

We must partner together with every other unit of

*ekklesia* in our locality. And this partnership must not have any denominational, traditional or cultural barriers.

It is absolutely vital that we understand this. I am not referring to an organisational unity, but to cross-forged spiritual unity. We cannot ignore the fact that we must be seen to be working together if we are to be evangelistically effective, if we are to grow.

The heart of the gospel is reconciliation, and unity is its essential expression. It is spiritually inconsistent to be passionate about church growth or evangelism and half-hearted about unity. This common attitude pours scorn on Jesus' John 17 prayer.

I am praying and working for the day when, in every district of London, there is a genuine partnership between the different church leaders and groups of believers.

This will be a partnership within which all the different congregations show their appreciation of all the other parts of the 'local church' by thanking God for them in their services, by sharing their pulpits, and by ensuring that there is never any public criticism.

It will be a partnership whose different parts agree to disagree about many things, but agree that they are one in Christ Jesus.

At the beginning of Revelation, when John sees his vision, he writes about seven lampstands. Each lampstand stands in an individual relationship to the lamp. Each has its own supply of oil. Each burns individually.

As Jesus gave seven personal messages to seven individual churches, every individual church must stand in an individual relationship with Jesus – and must shine separately as a local or community church.

However, the function of the lampstand is to bring the lights together so that they can shine together with a greater brilliance. Jesus is standing in the midst of the lampstands. They are individually related to him yet corporately joined to him. This dynamic tension is a vital key to growth.

I strongly believe in the integrity of individual congregations. They are governed individually by Christ. But they must stand together to express his body.

We can see this in the seven messages of Revelation. Jesus gave a separate prophetic word to each of the seven local churches in the Roman province of Asia. There was a special, personal revelation to each local or city church, but the constant exhortation of the Spirit was, 'Hear what the Spirit is saying to the churches'.

Other local or city churches were also to hear what God was saying. There was not one message for the whole church, but seven messages for seven particular city churches. Yet every expression of the church was meant to be aware of what God was saying to all the other churches.

This meant that there was both a prophetic individuality and a corporate application of what was said. This is the sort of helpful balance we should seek to establish in all our inter-church relationships.

## BACK TO BASIC BIBLICAL FUNCTIONS

Growing churches need to be as strong as possible in every area of their calling. It is not enough for us to say that our congregation is going to specialise in one particular area. We should not say, 'Let someone else concentrate on evangelism, we are going to focus on worship', or, 'Somebody else must get involved with pastoral care, we are spiritual warriors in this church'.

As I will show in chapter three, I believe that every expression of the church needs to know which group of people it is aiming to reach. Within a local network of churches, the whole community is best reached by each congregation targeting a particular section of the community. Despite this, every church must have a balanced ministry if it is to grow, if it is to reach its target people-group effectively.

It seems to me there are five basic functions which every expression of the church is called to fulfil.

## The Chinese Community Church

In 1985, my parents retired from the catering business and moved to London. We were young in the faith and on fire for God. As my parents spoke little English, we tried to find a Chinese charismatic church; but were not successful. In the end we settled at Kensington Temple. Although my parents could not understand the language, they enjoyed the presence of God in the services.

We spent two happy years at KT and won a number of Chinese people to Christ. But they spoke little English, found it difficult to participate in the services, and we lost contact with many of them.

The situation was serious, so – in September 1988 – fifteen of my friends and family started a satellite church for Chinese people. We called ourselves *'Salvation for Chinese Church'* and looked for a place in the centre of London. The Great Russell Street YWCA was the cheapest that we could find.

The early years were very painful. There were numerous problems. Myself and the core group were young, inexperienced and untrained in ministry. Most of us were in our teens and early twenties.

Although we were Chinese, some of us could not speak Cantonese very well and were not familiar with the culture. We looked Chinese, but were more English in our outlooks. It was not surprising that the Chinese community in

London did not take us seriously. For many months, the YWCA hall we used for our services was empty of people.

But we persevered, and began to learn how to reach the Chinese people. We concentrated on prayer and on personal and street evangelism. Little by little, people began to be won and there were over 60 adults in regular attendance by 1991.

At that stage, we divided into two services – an English speaking service which targeted young Chinese, and a Cantonese speaking service for the older generation. By 1994 the church had grown to over 130 committed members.

Every Pastor knows that things in a church are not always smooth. By the end of 1995 we had run into some internal conflict and the church lost many people. It was painful. We nearly lost our strength and motivation to continue.

But God was with us and we withstood the test. By the end of 1996 new people had joined and a full recovery had been made.

Our on-going vision is to continue to win Chinese people to Christ by evangelism and by church planting. We have now separated the English-speaking and Cantonese-speaking congregations. They now meet in different buildings and are developing into separate but related churches in the London City Church Network.

*Pastor Joshua Chan*

## Worship

The supreme call of the universal church is to worship God. Therefore, when we come together as distinct expressions we are supposed to make worship central.

If we want people to be in touch with reality, we must acknowledge God for who he is – the Creator and Redeemer of the whole world. We should worship Jesus for who he is – the eternal Son and Saviour of all humanity. And we should honour the Holy Spirit – our enabler and constant encourager.

Through our church worship, we should reflect on earth what the book of Revelation describes is already taking place in heaven. God seeks people who will genuinely worship him only in spirit and truth. This is a basic function of the church – and we must ensure that this happens in all our congregations.

It seems to me that worshipping in spirit and truth means allowing the Holy Spirit to bring his freshness, his life and his holy energy to our worship. It also means that we worship according to the truth of the biblical revelation about God – it means worshipping him as he really is, not as we imagine or would like him to be.

Our church worship should also be significant, meaningful, skilful and culturally relevant. God does not want our worship to be dull, repetitive or boring. He wants us to worship him creatively, in fresh, exciting ways which reflect his own creative nature and which inspire the people we are seeking to serve.

This is important because we find God through worship. He reveals himself when we worship and 'is enthroned on the praises of his people'. Praise and worship acknowledge God for who he is, and so much flows from this that we can often expect spiritual breakthroughs to occur when we are worshipping.

Worship should be high on the agenda in our churches, and we will not grow unless our worship is good. I believe that we must offer God the best from our culture. Every community church has to decide what this means for themselves, but I think that God deserves a richness of praise which uses many different styles of music.

## *Word*

The church is the custodian of eternal truth – the written word of God. Across the world, there are many rival claims to the truth; and, here in Europe, we live in a post-modern culture which denies the concept of absolute truth. Therefore the church has a basic function of teaching and preaching the truth with the greatest possible care and clarity.

At the moment, the church needs to be especially careful to maintain an absolute devotion to God's word. We must ensure that no manifestations of the Spirit or directional emphases distract us from scripture. The eternal, written word of God must remain primary, and the 'visible words' of God – baptism and communion – must be given their right places.

If a church wants to grow, I believe that every aspect of its life must be rooted in scripture. Every one of its ministries must be based in biblical principles. Every member must be constantly encouraged to subordinate their thinking to God's word. New converts who come into the church often have no biblical background and a great mass of contrary human ideas. It is urgent that they are quickly taught the eternal principles of grace and faith.

## *Witness*

Witnessing is another one of the church's basic functions. We are called to be Christ's witnesses – in word, in deed and in lifestyle. This is the evangelistic life of the church. In my experience, churches explode with growth when all the people are equipped and released as witnesses.

All churches have some members who naturally invite their friends and neighbours to services, gather people in, and bring their family along. It may be that they have a particular gift in this area, but how we wish that everybody was like them! If we want to grow, we must teach our congregations to do the same thing – to be involved in friendship evangelism and live as lively witnesses of Jesus.

Churches which do not burn with a passion for mission miss the whole point of their calling – to go and make disciples. Too many churches seem to think that Jesus charged them with holding meetings and waiting for people to come to them. But the church is called to go.

Of course, we need the guidance of the Spirit to find appropriate ways of witnessing which reach our generation and culture: I examine some of these in chapter six.

But, ultimately, the most effective witnesses are believers who live the ordinary dedicated life of Jesus, and gossip the good news in language that the people around them understand. We must show our people that this is what being a Christian really means. Before we can grow, there must be a strong evangelistic function which equips the whole church to witness.

## *Welfare*

Another basic function of the church is to provide pastoral care within the church, and community care outside the church. Some churches are so evangelistic that they do not care properly for their new converts. While others are so caring that they have no converts to look after!

We need to find a balance and ensure that the people in our churches are properly pastored. This does not mean only a visit when someone is ill or bereaved; it may mean the sort of caring recorded in Acts 6. In fact it was this sort of generous, practical caring which caused the early church to grow so fast and so far!

I believe that it is time for evangelism and pastoral care to come together, but especially *outside* the church. Too many charismatic conferences in the nineteen eighties modelled the idea that Christian meetings were the place for ministry. Jesus did call us all to be ministers, to be servants. But our first calling is to serve the community in which we have been placed. Ministry in meetings has a far lower biblical priority than ministry in the community.

This will be a major emphasis in growing churches. We

should be asking God how we can serve the people around us – especially as society disintegrates and social needs multiply. But remember, our motive must be simply to serve. We have been called to love, so our service must not be a means to an end.

Of course, we serve to the glory of God and in a way that we hope prompts some people to want to know Jesus. But our service must be pure, not manipulative. It must be a genuine outpouring of Christ's love.

We must be careful not to over-reach ourselves, to commence projects that we cannot carry through. But if we take care of the sick, the elderly, the broken-hearted, the imprisoned, the immigrants, the homeless, the handicapped, and so on, people will know that Jesus is alive and living in his church. It is no coincidence that revivals have often occurred when the church has been most deeply involved with social needs.

### *Warfare*

In Matthew 16:18, Jesus states that the gates of hell will not prevail against the church. The keys of the kingdom have been given to us. We are to bind and loose. This relates primarily to doctrinal purity and church discipline, but it also applies to spiritual warfare.

We will not be able to do the work of Jesus without grappling with those spiritual forces which are opposed to God's kingdom. By their very nature, growing churches will always be caught up in some element of warfare.

At one level, almost every aspect of worship, witness, welfare, proclaiming and listening to the word are acts of warfare. But there is also a direct, confrontational, intercessory aspect of warfare.

Growing churches will sometimes need to confront demonic powers through prayer, fasting and praise; but they will need to do it cautiously, under the direction of the Spirit – not rashly, twenty five times in every meeting!

In some churches, Satan has been bound so many times that the millennium should have been here six times over by now! We have to ask ourselves what we are

achieving by this. Warfare prayer is one of the church's
basic functions. It is high on God's agenda. But we must
always be clearly directed by the Spirit and according to
the word in everything we do.

## THE ONLY FOUNDATION

There is nothing particularly special or demanding about
being committed to church growth. All we are doing is
aligning ourselves with the vision and purpose of God. It
is Christ's work. He is the one who is essentially responsible for growing his church.

In Matthew 16:18, he promises, 'I will build my church'.
I find this enormously encouraging. He does not ask me
to build it. He does not ask you to build it. It will come
about through *his* power, *his* effort, *his* energy and *his*
resources.

There is, of course, something for us to do. We are
expected to co-operate together and with him. But the
main burden is entirely upon his shoulders.

He will provide us with everything we need to carry
out his work. He has already given us his Spirit. And he
will give us all the gifts and ministries which are needed
to build his church in our locality.

The challenge of Matthew 16:18 is, 'What are we building?' Are we building *our* church? Are we developing a
personal empire? Are we in competition with other leaders? Are we the spiritual counterparts of secular entrepre-
neurs? Or are we extending the kingdom of God and
seeing *his* church built?

As far as I can see, there is only one acceptable reason
why we should ever want to see churches grow: and that
is because it is Jesus' vision. It is his church. We are doing
his work. We are stewards of his possession. There is
nothing that we claim as our own. He is the head of every
expression of the church, and giving it back to him means
speedier and longer-lasting growth.

Many British churches are weak and ineffectual. 90% of
the population rarely, if ever, attends church. This grim

situation means that we need a clear vision of the finished product and a deep understanding of the position from which we work.

In Matthew 16:18, Jesus promises that we will prevail. Church growth is not an illusion. It is not an impossible goal. It is something which is fixed in the eternal purposes of God and has been ratified by the words of Jesus.

Jesus' promise to build his church is firmly established in the centre of the eternal purposes of God. It is not a side issue which God occasionally overlooks and only remembers when he is less busy.

Building his church is his number one priority. That is why we are here, and that is why we start from a position of accomplishment and victory. We have been given the simple responsibility of pushing back the powers of darkness, administering the victory in Jesus' name, and watching Jesus go on building his church.

Jesus' statement in Matthew 16:18, 'I tell you that you are Peter, and on this rock I will build my church' has caused considerable theological dispute. But most of the dispute is mere fancy, for Jesus could not have built on Peter as he never builds on any human person. It is Christ's church. It rests on the foundation of God.

When Jesus said, 'You are Peter', he used the Greek word *petros* – which means a small stone. But he then continued, 'On this rock I will build my church' – and used the word *petra* which means bedrock.

In this wordplay, Jesus is contrasting Peter with the real foundation, but he involves Peter by saying that he will give him the keys of the kingdom. Jesus is the bedrock, the real foundation, but God gives the keys to the little stones – to men and women.

The church is built entirely on him, on Jesus. Our part is simply to use God's keys to open the doors and welcome people in, and to lock doors with God's keys to keep the enemy out.

Whenever we consider church growth, we must remember that Christ is the only foundation on which we can build anything worthwhile. We do this in a similar way to Peter in Matthew 16:16. When he confessed Jesus as the Christ, Jesus told him that this truth had come to him by way of revelation. And, by implication, Jesus promised that his church would be built by similar super-natural, God-given revelations.

Church growth is a supernatural work. The Spirit brings us a revelation about Jesus – that is God's exclusive work. Our responsibility is to live in partnership with God and to co-operate with him by using only the keys and other equipment that he gives. God's power is released as we do this, and the church begins to grow.

When I began in the pastoral ministry, I had all the usual difficulties and struggles of a young minister in a small congregation. But I will never forget the thrill of watching people grow spiritually through revelation. I preached my sermons, and one person would come to Jesus and another would say that the word had changed their life.

It really can be fun to partner with the Spirit, because he takes our feebleness and changes it into his strength. It is like watching a miracle take place. As we preach, one person believes, another is built up, lives are changed. As the revelation flows, Jesus builds his church.


## THE ULTIMATE RESULT

Ephesians 4 is one of the great biblical chapters, and con-tains a snapshot view of a wonderful heavenly vision – the glorious end-time church.

It is such an encouragement to church leaders to know Jesus promises that he will complete what he began so long ago. He will establish a biblical church. He has been working on it throughout history, right up until now – the most exciting period yet in church history.

When Jesus returns for his bride, he will not come for an infant church but for a mature bride. He has promised that he will build his church, and this means he will com-plete his task.

Christ's body, the church, is God's agent or representative in the world. This means that Christ's work on earth can be carried out only through his body. When it is not a mature, strong and healthy body, the work of Christ is not done. But when the body is strong, and growing towards maturity, then God's work on earth can be accomplished.

In Ephesians 4:11-16, Paul writes about the church attaining the fullness of Christ. This means that, one day, the church will perfectly reveal Christ in all his fullness – right here *on earth*. This reinforces Paul's teaching in Ephesians 1:23, where he describes the church as 'the fullness of him'.

Paul makes it plain that Jesus has given apostles, prophets, evangelists, pastors and teachers to the church so that they will knit all God's people *together* for the work of service. It is this which builds up Christ's body and causes it to grow. According to Paul, these leaders are to go on with their work, building the church up for growth by building it together, until some wonderful things occur.

## *Unity*

Paul promises that the mature church will reach the unity of the faith. This is not the unity of the Spirit which began at the cross and so already exists, but unity in the essential doctrines of the faith and maturity of understanding.

This does not mean that all Christians will believe exactly the same things about everything, but rather that there will be strong unity in all the essentials of the faith throughout the true church – the genuine body of Christ.

It will be a unity within diversity – each expression of the church will still own and benefit from its distinctive emphases. And it will be a unity which brings a maturity of Christ in character – for the things which presently divide us are essentially our immature character and our immature understanding.

### Full knowledge

The fullness to come is the full knowledge of the Son of God. This will not be merely an improved version of our current knowledge; it will be *full* knowledge. This has to be the practical realisation of Jesus in his church.

In Philippians 3:8-16, Paul longs to know Christ, and the power of his resurrection, and the depth of his sufferings. And in Philippians 2:5-11, he urges us to make the mind of Christ our own. Can we imagine what the church will be like when we rise to this full knowledge? We will know Jesus in depth, and will experience his reality in every part of church life.

### Full stature

This is the heart of maturity. The mature church will form the perfect Person. We will be of full stature, fully mature. No longer will we be children, tossed one way or another, but strong and mature in Christ.

The church we read about in Acts is the infant church. The end-time church will be a mature, adult, vigorous church. If the early church was able to achieve so much, what will the end-time church accomplish? I am sure that the coming biblical church will see a massive outpouring of the Spirit which will lead to effective world-wide evangelism and unprecedented church growth.

### Christ's fullness

Finally, the mature church will be filled with the complete fullness of Christ himself. This means that we will be so full of Jesus that we can accurately represent him in the world and achieve everything he has asked.

This will be a church which manifests the fullness of his power, his wisdom, his love and his authority. We will show the world the fullness of his grace and holiness. Christ will be fully manifest both in us and through us.

The result will be a body of credible active witnesses throughout the entire world, in every nation and culture.

Surely this is a vision worth working towards, a dream

worth living for. Even the smallest step taken towards this is infinitely valuable. It will not be attained just by pastors and leaders, but by all Christ's body working together under his headship and power.

When we are caught up in the detail of our work, it is often helpful to step back and examine the full picture. There is a story of Sir Christopher Wren, who built St. Paul's Cathedral in London. While the building was going on, he disguised himself and visited the building site.

He asked one man what he was doing. The man replied, 'I'm building this wall'. He went further on and asked another worker what he was doing. This man said, 'I'm helping Sir Christopher Wren build the finest cathedral in the world'.

Every now and then, we need to step back from our small corner of God's building project and glimpse the whole structure and the final plans. We are building the finest building ever, and we are partnering in this with the Lord Jesus Christ.

The church is going to grow, and it can happen through every single reader of this book. Your expression of the church can grow. The church in your area can function as a biblical local church. Jesus has promised you that *he* will bring it about.

# QUESTIONS

1. How can you help your church to focus its thinking and speaking about 'the Church' more on people than on buildings and/or meetings?

2. What practical differences should it make to your church to think of itself as a community church rather than as a local church?

3. How can you help the people in your church to develop and express *koinonia* within the universal church *and* within the local church *and* within the community church?

4. Which function – worship, word, witness, welfare or warfare – does your church most emphasise? Which of these functions does it least emphasise? What action is needed to bring a better balance to your church's ministry?

5. How can you help the people in your church to grasp God's glorious destiny for the Church?

6. Why did your church start? What do most members think is the real reason for its present existence? What should its purpose be?

7. What changes do you need to implement as a result of the teaching in this chapter?

## TWO

# God wants your church to grow

Kensington Temple is known as one of Britain's largest churches, but our considerable growth cannot be separated from our strategy of planting as many small groups and new congregations as possible. I know that churches must not be judged by their size, and every small congregation in the London City Church Network knows just how deeply they are appreciated.

I also recognise that, in rural areas, a church with a numerically small congregation commonly forms a much larger proportion of its community than its more fashionable city or suburban counterparts.

For example, a village church with a congregation of 50 drawn from a village of 2,000 people will be making a similar impact on its community as an urban congregation of 1,250 drawn from a town of 50,000 people – and as a city congregation of 50,000 in a city of two million.

If such a large city church existed in Britain, we would know about it, and would classify it as successful. Yet thousands of small village churches already exist. Most of us know little about them and may be tempted, at times, to dismiss them as unimportant or insignificant.

## Small churches, large impact

However, where it matters, within their local communities, many of these 'small' rural churches are making a greater impact for the gospel than 'large' town and city churches.

The congregations of small churches tend to be drawn from their immediate community, whereas larger churches usually attract numbers from a wider geographic area. This means that many Christians neglect their own community in favour of the 'celebration' atmosphere of a large church.

In a village, most can identify some of the believers. The local people know where the minister lives and where the church building can be found. It is not the same in urban areas. For example, in London we find that most people do not know where the churches are, they cannot name the ministers, and they rarely know where any believers live.

## Small churches, deep fellowship

Small churches can also provide an amazing depth of fellowship and can offer the strength of intimate relationships.

In a large inner city church like Kensington Temple, many people come who do not want intimacy. They are hurting and looking for the anonymity of the crowds. We give it to them for a while, but we pray that they will be healed and teach them to seek this healing.

We say, 'Many of you who have come are hurting and want to hide. That's fine. Keep on hiding. But the time will come when you will be healed and put in a place of usefulness in the body.' That is when we encourage them to be involved with one of our smaller congregations which is trying to reach their particular community or people-group.

Church is all about people and relationships. There is a much greater opportunity in smaller churches to help people find and develop their ministries, as the whole church can be involved in ministry.

It is difficult to create intimate relationships and release everyone into ministry in a large church which focuses its activities on large meetings. Those of us who lead large churches need to develop structures which enhance fellowship and evangelism so that people are central to what we do. But the 'spectator' mentality (which is essentially alien to the biblical idea of church) can never be fully overcome in large meetings – or in large churches without breaking down into small groups.

## *The day of small things*

Zechariah 4:10 says, 'Do not despise the day of small things'. It was a time of restoration after seventy years of exile. A new temple was being built, but the people who supposedly remembered the glory of the old temple wept hypocritically. For them, the small new temple was a disappointment. It was just not good enough.

Too many people still look back at the past to some glory which was supposed to exist. Most often, it did not exist – at least not in the way they remember.

It is the same in the spiritual realm. People look back, but they will not look forward – and so they despise what they have. Even though the building in Zechariah's day did compare unfavourably with Solomon's temple, it was a significant restoration. So, today we must not despise our 'day of small things'.

Secular pressures encourage us to worship success, size and achievement. Yet God asks us to look deeper, beyond the appearance, to see the heart and the reality.

As we will see later, much supposed church growth has been merely a movement of believers from smaller congregations to more fashionable large ones. But it is not true church growth when one congregation grows at the expense of others. The real 'local' church has remained the same size. It is simply that the ecclesiastical pack has been reshuffled.

## The day of small egos

Habakkuk 3:17 states that, 'Even though there is no blossom on the trees, no fruit on the vine, yet will I rejoice in the Lord'. As leaders, we must rejoice in Christ whatever the size of our congregation. The egos of too many leaders are tied to the attendance at their services. This is highly manipulative and desperately immature.

If the leader's joy is not in Jesus, the congregation will be able to manipulate him or her – as they know that the leader fears their absence. We should rejoice in the Lord no matter what fruit we see – because our joy should be in him, not in our achievements.

Despite all this, it is important we remember that, whatever a church's size, regardless of whether it is expressed as a number or a percentage, God wants that church to grow.

## Breaking into growth

Some pastors have been leading churches for many years and still have not broken through into growth. We cannot be content with this. We must look for the hidden causes and tackle the real issues of stagnation.

Please never forget that God wants people to be attracted to his church. He does not want us to lose even one person from the church. I know that we must deal with sin and whatever hinders God's work, but some leaders are so preoccupied with these matters they seem to think that God has equipped them to empty churches!

Whenever we think about growth, we must not lose sight of the immense value God places on every single member in our church. We may have only fifteen, twenty, twenty-five or thirty people, but we must attend to every detail of their care and their enabling. We must appreciate each individual person and grasp their remarkable potential in Christ.

I suspect that this is why, at first, God graciously gives leaders small churches to care for. If we have taken care of the small things, when we grow large we should know that people – and only people – are what matter.

## GOD WANTS YOUR CHURCH TO GROW IN SIZE

We know that we must value smaller churches, and that we must be grateful for what God is doing in our day. But we must never forget that God wants every expression of his church to grow.

I am not suggesting that God wants every small church to become numerically large or every large congregation just to keep on getting bigger and bigger. I know from my experience at Kensington Temple that real church growth is often best achieved when a congregation sends out groups of members to plant new churches.

Instead, I am saying that it is God's will for every expression of his universal church – every local church, every community church, every cell group – continually to win new converts and to attract them into committed fellowship within the church.

### *Reaching the lost*

God wants us *always* to be reaching out to the lost in our community. Some churches get so involved in internal affairs and activities they forget that their main purpose is to reach the overwhelming majority of people who are not in their church.

Crowds followed Jesus wherever he went. Time and again the gospels record how Jesus looked at the crowds and was moved by compassion. He saw them as sheep without a shepherd. He saw the people as burdened and in bondage. And he gave the church the task of reaching out to the crowds with his love.

First of all, as a church we must know the specific needs of our communities. Then we must be moved by the particular needs of the people around us. Finally, we must begin to reach out with Christ's compassion and make a loving impact on our local communities.

Jesus is always wanting to reach out to the lost, so we

## Immanuel Christian Centre

We began back in 1989 as a mid-week house-group of eight people meeting in my home. Most of us were part of Kensington Temple, but a few attended different churches in London.

During the next two years, the group grew to 25 people and we thought about dividing into two groups. However, everybody wanted to stick together. Finally, we had to do something – so we started an extra meeting on a Sunday at my home.

In January 1993, we decided to become 'a church' and started meeting at a local school hall. However, many members left us at this time as they did not want to stop being involved with the churches that they had been part of for many years.

At first, it was difficult. The school was costly to hire. We had no musicians and no musical equipment – so we sang unaccompanied and clapped. Many members found that they preferred the 'house-group' mentality of focusing on their needs to a 'church' attitude of focusing on others. Some, who had been happy in a home-group which was led by a women, suddenly became uncomfortable in a church led by a woman.

Within a short while we were down to 10 people. I felt that it all would have been far easier and much better if I had been born a man!

We started training the few dedicated members and improving our organisation and administration. We focused on reaching out to non-believers – especially to families nearby: those who had stayed with us were comfortable with this.

As our numbers rose, we started a membership class, visitation, home-care groups and proper pastoral care. We reached out to the community through a programme we called *Breadline Newham*.

By 1995, 100 adults were worshipping with us as part of the church. By the end of 1996, there were between 150 and 200 people at every service. 90% of these had been converted through our activities. Only a tiny handful joined us from other churches.

We have not seen any sudden church growth. We have not had a dramatic influx through a special meeting or activity. It seems to us that the increase has been slow, but consistent, through the day-to-day evangelism of our members.

We still meet in the same school hall, but we also rent three other premises in the area to help us reach out more effectively. This is very expensive.

I believe that collective prayer and fasting is the foundation of all we do. We meet to pray every week and distribute daily prayer points for all the members. It is through intercession that we have kept evangelism as our number one priority.

*Pastor Dunni Odetayint*

must be careful that most of our church's energy is not dissipated on internal activities. Our energy must mainly be spent in reaching out to gather new people in.

## A sign of life

God wants our churches to grow as this shows that they are alive. Growth is part of life; in fact, it is a basic evidence that life exists. One of the most distinctive factors which distinguishes a living organism from a dead or dying one is its ability to grow – and to reproduce itself.

When we look at the biological signs of life, we notice the ability to consume and feed, to produce waste and consume energy, to grow and reproduce. A car can do nearly all these things. It burns fuel, produces waste gases, uses energy, moves freely. But it cannot reproduce itself.

In the same way, there are many mechanical churches. People may devour the sermons and make a lot of noise, but there is no real life if there is neither growth nor reproduction.

If our church is not growing, we must ask ourselves some serious questions. Please recognise that these should not be despairing questions; rather they should be positive, practical questions like, 'Why are we not growing?', 'When did we stop growing?', 'Why did we stop growing?', 'Where is growth on our list of priorities?', 'What can we do to kick-start growth?' But we must be motivated enough to ensure that our answers are accurate and that they are implemented.

## A sign of quality

God wants his church to grow because growth is a sign of quality disciples. Some leaders pose quality and quantity as alternative options for churches. They say to me, 'Well brother, you may have a big church, but we have real quality disciples'.

I always want to ask them, why, if they are of such high quality, they are so unattractive! In my experience, quality always leads to quantity. If we have Christ-like believers, people are attracted to the church.

In John 15, Jesus talks about us bearing much fruit. He has commissioned us to go out and bear fruit, fruit that will last. Now fruit is essentially attractive. It looks good and it tastes good.

But fruit also contains seeds, it is that part of the plant which is responsible for reproduction. God made fruit to look and taste good so that animals would eat it, and – in so doing – would carry the seed away so that another plant develops somewhere else.

It is the same in the spiritual realm. Jesus says that we are meant to bear fruit. This means that we are meant to look good, to be spiritually attractive. We are meant to taste good, so that – after close contact – people keep coming back for more. And we are meant to pass on the seeds, so that new life starts to develop in those who are attracted and who enjoy the contact.

All this means that a quality disciple is one who is distributing seeds, one who is reproducing and leading others to Jesus. We all know that Jesus said, 'Follow me and I will make you fishers of men'. This notion of bringing others to Christ is absolutely central to the idea of discipleship. Quantity depends on quality. Quality leads to quantity. The two are inseparable.

In John 6:26, immediately after the feeding of the 5,000, Jesus spoke to the crowds who were enthusiastically following him after the miracle. He said, 'You are seeking me not because of the miracle but because of the bread'. He goes on to say, 'You were filled'. When we fill people today, they come. When we meet their needs, they come. When we give them good bread, they come.

I know that there can be a temptation to compromise in order to grow churches. However, some people who criticise large churches for compromising are actually criticising particular means of evangelism.

But if growth means putting, say, different music in the church, then I think that we should do it. When asked if he liked the style of music in his church, one London leader said, 'I hate it! But it's not for me, it's for them'. He was referring to those he was seeking to reach with the gospel.

This leader is a great theologian and a very conservative man, but he knows the importance of ignoring personal preferences in order to be more effective in reaching out to others. This is not bringing worldliness into the church; it is adapting a peripheral matter to be effective in the local culture.

### A sign of developing ministries

God also wants his church to grow because the process of growth involves many more people in ministry. I promise you that growth occurs whenever we equip people for ministry and release them into ministry.

Some leaders seem to like to control everything, to do everything, to be considered omni-competent and indispensable. But when, as leaders, we deeply apply Paul's teaching in Ephesians 4:11-12, growth is the inevitable result.

The different leadership ministries have one principle function: to equip the saints for the work of ministry – not to do it for them! Paul makes it clear that this is what builds up or edifies the church. (The Greek word that Paul uses here, *oikodome*, is the same word that Jesus uses in Matthew 16:18 when he promises to build his church.)

The principle purpose of leadership – whatever the size of the church – is to release people in ministry so that the church may be built. When we leaders do our job properly, I guarantee that the church really does start to grow.

### GOD WANTS TO USE YOU TO BRING GROWTH

Whatever our situation, no matter how small our congregation or how long it is since we saw growth, we should not despise what we have. If we give it to Jesus, he will cause it to grow.

In Exodus 3 & 4, when Moses was called by God to free the Israelites from Pharaoh, he said, 'I can't possibly do that!' But Moses had to relearn a lesson. He had spent the first forty years of his life thinking that he was somebody special, and the next forty years realising that he was nobody. Now he had to grasp what God could do through a nobody!

While Moses was protesting, God asked him, 'What's in your hand?' Moses replied that he was holding his shepherd's rod. 'Throw it on the ground,' God said. Moses did. It immediately turned into a snake and Moses jumped back.

God told Moses to pick up the snake. When he did, it turned back into a rod. From that moment on, it was no longer called the rod of Moses but the rod of God.

Moses then had to be convinced that God could work through his hands, and that God would help him speak and tell him what to say.

It is the same with us. God prefers to use those leaders who know that they are nobodies. He prefers to use those who know that they cannot achieve anything on their own, who are convinced that their natural abilities and training are inadequate for the task at hand.

God asks us today what we have in our hands. We know that we have next to nothing, but God says, 'Put it down. Lay it at the feet of Jesus.' In his hands, we find that whatever we have becomes something else.

In the rod, God gave Moses an instrument of great power. Through the rod, he delivered a nation – he led a people to freedom. Some wonder what the rod was made of, and how Moses held it. It was simply a rough wooden rod, but it was the instrument in God's hand.

## We have the resources

God chooses to use many different instruments – we see that in the story of the five loaves and two fish. The little that we have, given to Jesus, broken by him, can be multiplied into food for thousands.

The early church in Jerusalem began with 120 mem-

bers. They had no property, no social standing, no institutional backing, no finance, no models of ministry, no
training manuals or technological aids. Yet within three
years they had filled Jerusalem with their teaching.

So it is in all things. God has given us all something,
but do we know what it is? By the miracle of grace and
power, through his irrevocable call, we have the keys to
growth – to opening the church doors – in our hands.

You might not see it, know it or feel it. But, right now,
in your situation, you have all that you need to start growing. Please ask him to show you what the keys are for
your situation. I promise that you will find them within
your church: the people resources, the necessary talents,
the spiritual gifts, and the supernatural enthusiasm and
energy.

## *We must be faithful with our resources*

Church growth always starts in a tiny way – with just one
new person joining the congregation. But even before
that, it begins with us being faithful with – and grateful for
– the resources that God has given us.

The Scriptures highlight the importance of 'faithfulness
in small things' through Jesus' parables in Matthew 24:45
– 25:46.

In the first story, Jesus says that faithful, wise servants
will be found doing the master's will so that they are
rewarded when the master returns. Two qualities are
prized: faithfulness and wisdom. It is wise to fulfil whatever stewardship has been given to us – and to go on
doing it. Ultimately, the Lord always rewards such faithfulness.

In the third parable, the master gives talents to his servants according to their abilities. The servant who hid his
talent was wicked and lazy, but the others put theirs to
work and doubled them.

This suggests that the value of our ministry is not mea-
sured by the numbers who attend our churches. Rather, it
implies that we must be faithful according to what we
have been given.

In another parable, in Luke 16, Jesus commended a corrupt manager – not because of what he did, but because he was clever enough to use the little he had. In verse 10, Jesus says, 'He who is faithful in what is least is faithful also in much; and he who is unjust in what is least is unjust also in much'.

Jesus is saying that, if worldly people invest in worldly things to achieve worldly results, how much more should we invest in spiritual things to achieve spiritual results.

Although this parable is primarily about money, it also applies to every aspect of stewardship. I think that there is a deep spiritual principle here. If we are faithful with little then we will be faithful with much. If we are good stewards of what he has given us, we will be rewarded and will receive more. To him who has, more shall be given.

All this means that, as church leaders, we must begin where we are. We must not be frustrated by the difficulties of our situation or by its smallness in size. We must begin where we are and faithfully use the resources, talents, people and abilities that we have. If we do this, we will be rewarded and God will give an increase.

When I was a new believer, I was convinced that I was called to save the whole world. I asked God what I should do. The only revelation which came into my mind was that I was to pick up the hymn books from the church floor – but I knew that was a call from God.

In many ways, there is no difference between what I am doing now and what I was doing then. It is all service with and for Jesus – functioning in partnership with him. It is obeying what he tells us to do, and depending on his power to do it. Picking up hymn books one Sunday does not take much power, but it takes a lot to do it *every* Sunday.

We must never think or suggest that there is any difference between God asking us to pray for a person's healing and him asking us to pick up a hymn book. It is all just hearing and obeying.

If I had refused to pick up the hymn books, to be faith-

ful in the small things, I doubt whether God would be giving the increase that he is to our work in London today.

## GOD WANTS YOUR CHURCH TO GROW IN MATURITY

Until now, we have thought about church growth only in
terms of an increase in size. But to have a better understanding of the dynamics of church growth, we need to
appreciate that the life of any church can be likened to the
birth, growth and development of a human life.

If we want our church to break into numerical growth,
it is helpful to know what stage of development we have
reached. I have found that the immediate action we need
to take to kick-start numerical growth depends on the
stage of development that the church has reached.

I suggest that there are usually seven ages of any
church. I know that these are slightly artificial and arbi-
trary divisions, but they are useful in helping us to understand where we are as a congregation.

### *Conception – the beginning*

Every human baby must be conceived. It is the same with
every expression of the universal church.

Church conception occurs when the seed of the vision
comes into the mind of a leader. God plants this seed as
a holy vision, and places his call or burden on a leader or
group of people.

Perhaps they are challenged by a special need, or by a
village or urban area which has no church, or by a social
group in their community which is not being reached with
the gospel. They cry over a district or group and God
places his hand on them and whispers, 'This is for you.'

This is when the seed of the divine vision is sown and
given life. It is the moment when the church is conceived.
But it is not enough only to conceive. Just as so many
human conceptions miscarry, so many godly visions come
to nothing. Any vision must spend time growing, developing and becoming strong.

## *Gestation – private development*

Human babies spend nine months growing in their mothers' wombs before they see the light of day. Babies which are born prematurely are usually weak. They struggle and need special care. They are less likely to survive than those which go to term.

Every church needs a period of gestation, when the vision has a chance to grow before it is birthed in reality. It is good and necessary to dream privately before facing the difficulties of turning the vision into reality.

This is a very important stage. Many new churches die young, or struggle unnecessarily at first, because they were birthed too soon. The vision did not have long enough to develop and grow in safety.

The embryonic plans for a new church must spend time developing and being nurtured 'in the womb of the mother'. The vision needs to be clarified and focused through prayer, intercession and listening to God. Sensible research must be undertaken. Plans have to be formulated and tested. Tentative contacts and visits should be made.

Most natural mothers do not announce their pregnancy 'until they are sure'. Many keep the news private for as long as possible. Virtually all prospective parents break the news to close members of the family before widely announcing it. So it should be in the spiritual. We should allow the vision to develop within us before speaking about it publicly.

As time goes by, however, we can begin to mention the vision so that people can begin to identify with it. Some will hear God for themselves and express their commitment to the vision. Others, equally, will rightly realise that this is not God's vision for them.

If enough time is given to gestation 'in the womb', a group will emerge which knows that this is God's work for them. When they link together in prayer, the vision grows, gets stronger and develops quite naturally. But, as with human children, there must be a time for giving birth.

## Parturition – the birth

This is the exciting moment when the church is officially launched. Like the birth of a baby, this brings great joy, happiness and hope for the future.

When a church is born, those who gave birth have plans, expectations and vision. Every new church must have a tightly focused purpose and ethos. This is the basic God-given vision which was developed in gestation; it is the specific calling given by the Holy Spirit which everyone knows and subscribes to.

## Infancy and childhood – the early years

This is the fun stage of church development when the new church begins to find its feet. It starts to grow, stretch out and make mistakes.

We need to keep a sense of perspective at this stage, and be able to laugh at ourselves. Too many young churches are too earnest and too serious. Some try to use the format and style of large celebration meetings when they have twenty people in a small room!

In our experience, much of the joy in a new church comes from being under the supervision of a parent or guardian church. Within the London City Church Network, as we have been starting new community churches, we have found the benefit of new churches being supervised, advised, protected and encouraged by an older, larger church.

This parent/child relationship is based on love, commitment, prayer and support. I believe that this relationship is vitally necessary. We are not 'lone rangers' in the church. We are part of a family.

All human children need to grow up as part of a family if they are to develop identity, stability, security and maturity. It is the same with new churches. The parent/child relationships we have sought to develop in London do not mean oppression or domination; instead, they mean teaching, training, releasing, encouraging and enabling.

We have found it to be a mutually enriching relationship which gives the people involved in both old and new churches a sense of pride and purpose, as well as genuine security and stability.

## *Adolescence – the growth spurt*

This is the stage when the problems really begin! This is when a person or church develops a desire for its own identity. It wants to make its own place in the world. It is usually the stage when parents despair of their offspring.

Adolescent churches often want to break free from the parent church, to be a mature church in their own right, to have a totally independent identity.

It seems to me that most of the problems which come at this stage in church life are due to two things. They are caused either by over-authoritarian parents who need their offspring to remain dependent, or by a worldly desire for independence rather than a godly desire for mutual inter-dependence.

These sorts of tensions can lead to the ecclesiastical equivalent of a teenager running away from home! Most church splits occur at this stage, as one group tries to move on and another wants to stay in relationship with the parent.

It is important that both parent and child churches prepare for adolescence in advance. They need to understand the dynamics of the stage before it is passed through. Then they must shake off the immature wranglings and break through the difficult times into the sixth age of the church.

Adolescence is always a key stage for learning. However, this genuine hunger for learning can leave adolescent churches vulnerable to extreme and silly ideas or to a pre-occupation with peripheral matters.

Adolescence is also often the time of fastest growth. But rapid growth during this stage – like ravenous hunger for teaching – must not be mistaken for signs of maturity!

In fact, it is precisely when churches are growing at their fastest in adolescence that they most need the tactful and sensitive support and guidance of the parent church.

## *Maturity – the reproduction*

As God teaches us, allows us to make mistakes, and corrects us, so we can begin to take our place in society as a mature church. Every church has to pass through adolescence. We cannot avoid it or leap over it. We have to endure that time of struggling to reach a place of maturity.

Of course, mature churches do not get everything right! There will still be divisions and tensions, but the mature church – whatever its size – should function fully. It should be 'grown up' and beginning to equip others and give birth to other churches.

I do not want to stretch the analogy too far, or make an inappropriate comparison. However, please recognise that mature humans have been made for committed relationships with other humans who are different from them, who complement them and enable them to reproduce!

It seems to me that too many mature churches are involved in relationships with churches which are exactly the same as themselves. These may be satisfying and comfortable friendships, but they can be sterile relationships which do not facilitate reproduction.

Jesus' John 17 prayer shows that unity or 'oneness' is the basis of growth. For unity to be real, it must be unity in diversity: even the pagans unite with those they agree with.

I feel that this 'diversity within unity' is one of the greatest strengths of the London City Church Network. Many of our congregations are based in ethnic groups which have very different cultures. This does not affect just the way we dress and eat, but also the way we worship, preach, pray, train, think, fellowship and reach out.

Despite their differences, our community churches are committed to each other, to worshipping and working together, to helping and supporting each other. I am sure that the stimulation of these differences has been a significant factor in our growth.

One of the problems with human maturity is 'middle-age spread'. Mature churches know that they should not aim to be fat! God does not want obese churches; he wants reproducing churches. He wants mature churches which, like the heroes of Genesis 5, are still furiously begetting a multitude of sons and daughters in their ripe old age!

Although mature churches have their own distinctive place in the body of Christ, I feel that they still need the support and encouragement of relationship. Like any adult, it is still part of a family. It should not disown and disregard its family connections. Rather, it should take its equal place in society while still honouring its parents.

From Kensington Temple, we launched what is known as the London City Church. Churches are able to grow and mature within this. Eventually, they take their equal place alongside Kensington Temple as a parent church.

We see ourselves separately as many 'community churches' which are trying to reach different groups in London. And we also see ourselves together as one 'local or city church' in London. Of course, we recognise and make it clear that there are many other London churches which, with us, are part of Christ's one true church in London.

Although Kensington Temple is numerically the largest church in the London City Church Network, each church has an equal place within the network. All pray together, train together, celebrate together and work together to make London a place where Jesus is known.

As our new churches themselves increasingly initiate even newer churches, there is little that – alongside other city-wide churches – we cannot do with God in this great metropolis. Although maturity must be the goal for all churches, there is an acute danger that we may slide through it into an unproductive part of the seventh stage – old age.

## Perivale Community Church

In April 1993, I sat with Colin Dye talking about my future role in KT. He said that he wanted me to pastor a new church. For two hours, I explained why I should not and could not lead a church.

In the next two weeks, I applied for 16 teaching jobs – but got no replies. I also felt convicted over my wrong attitude! When I next met with Colin, he said that I should think about planting a new church, and I mentioned the possibility of planting one where I lived, in Perivale, West London. Colin announced this as fact at the next staff meeting!

The staff and congregation gave constant encouragement. Members were asked to attend the new church, and two elders joined the team. By the time we launched, in October 1993, 45 people were committed to the new work.

After one month, I was convinced that God was challenging us to plant a second church. KT leaders encouraged me to 'go for it'! By January 1994, we had 100 people attending – including children, so we launched a second church nearby that Easter with 25 adults. In the next 2 years it grew to 70 people.

For a while it was difficult at Perivale, as some of the people had left to start the new work. Numbers were down and the meetings were hard work. But, within six months, Perivale was stronger than before the church plant. This taught us a critical lesson.

God challenged me to plant two new churches from Perivale in 1995. This meant releasing key leaders to develop the new works. The first church began with 15 people – and reached 40 members in 2 years.

The second was more difficult. We found it hard to establish a core group, and considered cancelling the project. But we pressed on, and – a month after the launch – 20 people were attending. This has since risen to 30 people.

In the months after each plant, numbers were down at Perivale. Yet they just kept on rising back towards the 100 mark. It seems that God gives people back to us as quickly as we give them away.

In fact, we started a third church at the end of 1995. One of our house-groups was growing so quickly that we launched it as a church with 30 members.

By the beginning of 1996, we were back to 100 people at Perivale. This was exactly where we had been a year before, but we had started three flourishing congregations.

Three years after our launch with 45 people, there were 6 churches with over 300 people involved. This was only possible because of great support and encouragement from the LCC Network. And because our members have never lost the vision for planting churches – even when it looks as though we do not have enough resources for the job.

*Pastor Alistair Taylor*

## Old age

There is no other option for people but to get old and die. It does not have to be the same for churches, yet old age can creep in.

A church does not even need to be advanced in years before it becomes 'old'. Many quickly become static in their thinking. They think and live in the past. They say, 'It is not like it used to be', or, 'We never did it that way before'.

In a church's old age there is stagnation and complacency. Nothing is conceived or given birth to. There is little fresh vision. Rigidity and inflexibility set in. Activities are kept going only because someone would be upset if they were suspended – not because the activity is achieving very much.

Old age may be inevitable and irreversible for people, but the good news for churches is that we can continue to grow and give birth. We do not need to stagnate, and we can reverse the trend if we have stagnated. There is always an opportunity to change and discover fresh life.

Abraham found that, although he and Sarah were far past the normal age for reproduction, they could bring forth something fresh and new. Our God is the God of new things, and tired old churches can be reborn. Thank God that the promise in Psalm 92:14 is being experienced in many churches today.

In many societies, the elderly are esteemed and valued for their wisdom. Churches which have reached this level of maturity through the Spirit can retain their vision – or can conceive fresh vision – to stand alongside the wisdom that they have accumulated over the years.

Personally, I find it very enriching to be in a relationship with churches which are drawn from all these seven ages. Reinvigorated old churches have so much to offer to struggling new churches. Difficult adolescent churches stretch the faith and resources of mature churches. The transparent delight of baby churches helps other churches to stay young. I don't think that I could ever go back to being part of one independent congregation which was trying to work alone in its locality – it's much too dull!

These seven ages form an analysis of church development which can prove helpful, as it helps us to see where we fit in and where we need to make changes. The analysis can be applied both to the whole congregation and also to different parts or activities within the congregation.

Many of our church programmes go through these seven stages, and there can be a time when a project or activity needs to be buried! Most churches are good at starting things but not so good at ending them. Every now and then, we find it helpful to go through every area of our church life and ask if the programmes are still achieving the vision with which they began. Inevitably there are some things which have passed the point of usefulness.

One of the greatest tests of a leader comes when he or she realises that somebody's pet project should be closed down. How they handle this difficult situation often determines the church's direction, mission and growth for very many years to come.

## YOU HAVE TO PAY THE PRICE OF GROWTH

There is always a cost factor in growth. In ordinary life, we know that nothing of worth can be achieved without some sort of cost. In 2 Samuel 24:24, David said that he would not give 'to the Lord my God with that which costs me nothing'. In modern sport, there is the popular phrase, 'No pain, no gain'. And in church growth we must be ready to be stretched further than we thought possible and to pay the considerable price of growth.

### *Facing facts*

Church growth tests in the United States at the end of the 1980s discovered that – although they had grown a number of large churches – there was still roughly the same number of Christians at the end of the decade as there had been at the beginning. All that had happened was a reshuffling of Christians around different churches.

A similar pattern has been observed in some rural areas of Britain. One particular church in a small market town grows dramatically. It looks like church growth, but a close examination shows that the growth comes from two sources. Firstly, there are believers who left small churches in the surrounding villages and started to travel to the larger 'celebration' style church. And, secondly, there are believers who moved into the area and were attracted to the large church instead of being scattered among many small churches as in the past.

Not only has there been little genuine growth in these cases, but also the Christian community and witness in the villages has been greatly impoverished.

Even where, as in some British towns, the wider church in the locality has grown numerically, individual churches have often rejoiced prematurely. They have not looked behind the growth to see that their increase has only reflected the rise in the general population through housing developments. Is it really church growth if a congregation of 150 in a town of 60,000 grows to 200 when the town grows to 80,000?

All this has caused many church growth theorists to think again, and to ask themselves, 'How are we going to ensure that we win new converts?' In the United States, this has sparked a great move of God in intercession and a desire to plant new churches.

Gradually, church leaders have come to recognise that the planting of new churches actually releases growth. As a general trend, new churches do not grow by attracting existing believers from established churches – they grow by converts. And when believers move into an area, they tend to join established churches rather than young churches.

Obviously, people will sometimes join new churches from other churches – especially if they are already living in the new church's target group or area. But, generally, it really does appear that small young churches have a greater tendency to win new people to Jesus than larger, old churches.

For example, an established congregation of 300 is likely to grow mainly by attracting believers who move into the area and discontented believers in other churches. It will probably feel comfortably full at most services. Much of the energy will be focused on the needs of the congregation. It is unlikely to be that attractive to minority groups in the community.

But imagine what might happen if – after much prayer and consideration of the possible consequences – that same church decided to give birth to two new churches each with fifty members. These could be targeted at some groups in the community that the parent church had not been reaching effectively; perhaps a poor council estate, a particular ethnic group or an edge-of-town affluent commuter development.

The parent church would probably feel half-empty at most meetings and some leaders might fear the death of 'mother'. However, there would be a real buzz of excitement in the church as reports came in of progress and setbacks. Members of the parent church would feel excited and stimulated by what was going on through them – and this would have a positive effect on their own church. There would be an inevitable switch to evangelistic prayer and action to fill the empty spaces.

Furthermore, the new churches would start to reach groups with the gospel that the parent church could never have reached in depth. Very many more people would be released in ministry. An exciting and stimulating network of relationships would develop.

At a superficial level, it might not look like church growth for a few years. A large church would have reduced in size and few people would know about the others. But I suspect that, in three years time, there would be many more new converts than if the established church had not taken the risk of sending out some of its people. And the benefits of a large congregation would be retained when the three churches come together for times of celebration.

Of course, the leaders would need to ensure that they

did not drain the 'mother' church of all its key leaders – and that they did not use the process to get rid of difficult members!

However, our experience at Kensington Temple is that this sort of process – when planned carefully, prayed through thoroughly and carried out slowly – greatly facilitates genuine church growth both in the main congregation and in the newly planted churches. It is a real sign of hope to me that this pattern of growth is increasingly being adopted all over the world.

It can often be a painful process to look at the objective facts concerning our churches. Testing growth levels can be a painful exercise, but it must be done. Churches must be surveyed as they really are, not as we think they are or wish them to be.

The problem becomes worse when leaders explain away or make excuses about the smallness of their churches or their lack of new converts. We need the courage to acknowledge when something is wrong, to identify the problem and to deal with it.

I am not suggesting that we should grab the latest gimmick. Instead, we should dive deeply into the Scriptures to determine how we can lead our churches into the growth Christ intends.

### Facing fears

Every leader knows what it means to struggle with fears: 'I can't. I'm afraid. I'm inadequate. I'm no good. Everybody else can do it better than me.' We must rid ourselves of such negative and inaccurate thinking.

No matter how much we are involved with the church, any success is nothing to do with our ability. It is a matter of God's power, and our sufficiency is from him. The fear of failure must not prevent us from going forward.

There are two kinds of failures: those who have tried and failed, and those who have never tried. Failure is not a problem. But not attempting something for God is a huge problem. It is far, far better to try and fail than not to try at all.

In fact, I think that it is sometimes better to fail than to succeed. If we fail and learn from our mistakes we can be more effective the next time. But if we succeed and don't know why, we can proceed with arrogance and a lack of self-awareness.

Many of us are afraid of what people will think, but Proverbs 29:25 says that this brings a snare to us. We overcome this fear by depending on the word of God rather than on our own confidence.

Some of us are afraid of hard work. We all want things to happen easily. Yet hard work is often the only difference between success and failure. It is one thing to know what should be done, and another to put all the necessary energy into it – and to do it without giving up. Many of us are not doing the wrong things at all in our churches; we just need to persevere a bit more.

A few of us are frightened of commitment. It is demanding both to lead a church and to be involved in planting a new church. It usually takes about five years to establish a new congregation – and we need to be prepared to make this the priority in our lives. We must not give up when we are discouraged or tempted to move elsewhere.

Western society is an increasingly uncommitted environment. There is less and less commitment both at work and in the family. We need to resist this in the church. We need to spell out the cost of establishing new churches and the pastoral commitment it requires. The Bible says that shepherds must lay down their lives for their sheep, and we do this by living them out as servants.

Perhaps the biggest fear we face is that of leaving the comfort zone. Every leader faces an almost demonic choice. It is as if the devil says, 'I've noticed you. You've got a great ministry, but let me make a suggestion. Don't push too much on missions and only evangelise occasionally'.

The deal is this: if we don't bother the devil, he won't bother us! We will have a fairly comfortable life. He will give us enough misery to make us look like real leaders, but not too much to make our lives too unbearable. It is called compromise. And it is very serious.

We must not give in. We must face this fear with the confidence that God's perfect love casts out all fear. Faith will destroy the fear, because there is a far better fear to live by. This is the fear of standing before Jesus knowing that he will gently ask us what we have done with the talents he gave us.

## Facing obstacles

Once we have faced the facts and dealt with our fears we can get on with the task of being a co-worker with Christ as he builds his church. But no sooner do we start than we have to face all sorts of obstacles. And removing them is costly.

Anybody with anything other than a 'maintenance mentality' will be confronted with obstacles. We meet opposition essentially when we try to do something different. 'It can't be done. It hasn't been done. We've tried it before and it doesn't work here.'

There are always obstacles within the church which prevent growth taking place. We have to face these obstacles and remove them. I know that this is very hard in most churches as some of the most straightforward changes can cause the greatest division.

All hell can break loose when we suggest removing the pews, or swapping the piano for a synthesiser. These things may seem trivial, but they cause problems which must be handled firmly and sensitively.

The obstacles do not only come from the congregation, I have often found that the leader's favourite theories or themes can also be a blockage to growth.

No matter how precious our ideas are to us, if they don't work we need to accept their barrenness, finish with them, and find something that does.

Sometimes our style is wrong. It needs to be changed. At other times it is our approach. We must find another one. It is remarkable how adaptable we leaders can be when we really make up our minds!

There was a time at Kensington Temple when we had to face the facts about a particular training programme. We started with one person who was a trainee pastor. To maximise the time together we gave the young man a small salary, and within a few months there were ten people on the programme.

Each time we added someone to the programme we increased our expenditure. Soon we had applications for twenty people and were overspending. Something had to be done very quickly.

We went through the entire church ministry, and nobody wanted to change the training programme because it was such a valuable resource. However, I realised that we had to make adjustments. We turned it into a part-time programme, and the trainees now have to work to support themselves and pay a fair price for the training.

Before we dealt with this obstacle, the more we trained the less we could afford to do. After we had dealt with it, the more we trained the more we can afford to do. Now we have over three hundred people in training who are all supporting themselves.

It is critical that we learn to identify the obstacles which are preventing growth. At times we may be too close to the work to be able to see the problem and will need the help of other leaders who can come and visit. Sometimes the Spirit will give us a flash of inspiration which makes the difficulty plain. Many times we are only too aware of the obstacle, the real problem is our fear of dealing with it!

It seems to me to be important that – right from the outset – people understand the overall vision and appreciate the steps which are needed to reach that vision. The changes can then be explained within the context of that vision. Even if people do not like the changes, at least they can see why we are making them. It is because we are committed to reaching more people with Jesus' love and grace.

Of course there are much greater obstacles to growth than Victorian pews. For example, one new church that I was involved in planting felt that God wanted them to minister to the outcasts and wounded of the community – and a couple started attending with enormous social, moral and spiritual problems.

They were a very demanding and unwilling couple, and they wore out the leadership with constant telephone calls and a succession of crises. They were an overwhelming drain on the resources of the small church.

As a result of getting involved with this couple, the church of 40 people were drained and deflected from their real task of building up the fellowship.

If a fraction of the time used in helping this crisis couple had been used in evangelism and growing as a church, the church would have been stronger to help problem people. The church was simply not equipped to deal with the couple at this stage in its development. It would have been better for us to say 'We are sorry we cannot help you' and to have referred them to some agency which could help.

In the next section I will set out some practical keys which can open our church doors to growth, and each one of these involves dealing with an obstacle.

Radical changes are required in both attitude and detail if we are to see substantial church growth through conversions in our generation. If we want to experience the joy of church growth, we must be ready to endure the pain of the price of that growth.

# QUESTIONS

1. What size is your 'community church' as a percentage of the population in your area? What size is your 'local church' as a percentage of the population in the area? How much do you realistically expect these percentages to grow in the next three years?

2. Which stage have you reached in the seven ages of a church?

3. How many new converts have been added to your church in the last two years? Is this a satisfactory level of growth? What would be satisfactory?

4. What are the specific resources which God has given your church to help it grow? Which of these are not being used and which are being misused?

5. What are the three main obstacles to growth in your church? How should they be overcome?

6. What are your main fears about church leadership and growth? How should you deal with them?

7. What practical steps would be needed for your church to plant a new church?

## THREE

# Getting the vision right

By now, we have got to grips with some basic biblical ideas about the church. We have understood that God wants every expression of his church to grow. We have seen that smaller churches have an important place in God's kingdom. Now it is time to examine the practical and spiritual details which help a small church to grow.

It seems to me that there are three main keys to growth; and we must use them all, not choose between them. In this chapter, we will see that the first key is to receive, develop and constantly explain God's clear vision and direction for the church.

In the next two chapters we will see that the other keys are attending to all the small details and ensuring that people are central to all we do and think.

If we want to breakthrough into significant growth, we will not choose between these three keys. We will grasp them all together and hold them in balance.

### A military attitude

Before introducing the first key, I want to encourage all Christian leaders and workers to develop a strong and almost military attitude towards church growth.

This means avoiding those things which have nothing

72

to do with the real battle. All Christian workers have legitimate civilian pursuits which have no place when they are soldiers at war. Too many believers are more concerned with their pot plants than with praying and passing on the good news.

We must resist the danger of creating a 'cosy nest' mentality rather than an 'army barracks' attitude. We are disciples. We are soldiers at war. Of course, even soldiers have time off for rest and recreation, but they can never forget that they are soldiers on active service.

Christian leaders should not neglect the important truth that their churches are at war, and the central war-time question is, 'Who is going to win?' We began this book with the confidence of Jesus' victory, but we have to translate that victory into church growth through conversions in our locality. That must be our main pre-occupation, and the chief purpose in life of every member of our churches.

## WHAT IS OUR VISION?

Growth always starts with vision. It is no good leaping ahead and tinkering with tiny details, arranging special meetings or planning new programmes unless the vision is in place.

We will not kick-start growth by introducing modern hymns, removing pews or opening a youth club – *unless* these are essential and unavoidable steps towards realising God's vision. The vision must come first. All the practical details must stem from the vision and fit in with the vision.

But first of all, we need to know what vision is, how we arrive at a vision, how we check our church's vision and how we implement a vision.

Proverbs 29:18 states that, 'Where there is no vision the people perish'. The NJB translation more correctly states, 'the people get out of hand'.

Without natural vision, we lose direction and cannot see where we are going. Most of us dread losing our vision more than any other sense. We visit an optician when we suspect that our sight is failing. If necessary, we start wearing glasses which are specially made for us.

When we need to improve our vision, only a fool grabs a pair of glasses which have been prescribed for another person. Yet that is what happens in the spiritual realm.

Leaders see a vision which works for another church; they 'borrow' it, try to apply it to their own situation, and then wonder why it does not work for them!

In John 14:4, Jesus says to the disciples, 'Where I go you know, and the way you know'. Astonishingly, after so long with Jesus, the disciples replied, 'Lord, we do not know where you are going, and how can we know the way?'

I wonder how many modern disciples really know where Jesus is going in their community, and what the way forward is for their church. Perhaps we should own up if we are unclear about where, in particular, Jesus is taking our church. Before we try to move off, we must always spend time discovering God's way forward.

Time and again, I am asked how to revive a dying church. My answer is always the same, 'Get the vision right'. It may seem that 'rigor mortis' has set in, but God's prophetic vision can resuscitate any dying church.

### A vision which is clear

I know that God can bring fresh vision into any church. His vision can be lifted up before the congregation so that the people no longer look at themselves or the pastor. Their eyes can be lifted higher. Even the most discouraged believers can be united and filled with hope when they see God's vision for their church.

Vision is not a kind of vague dream about what we would like to happen if things improved or new people joined the church. Nor is it human wishful thinking or a good idea picked up in a book!

Holy vision identifies the goal that we are aiming at. It establishes the destination we are travelling towards. It determines the purpose of all our activities. God's vision

should be the arbiter of all our decisions and programmes.

Habakkuk 2:2 says, 'Write the vision down, make it
clear, make it plain, so that a herald may run with it.' I
believe that our vision must be clear, simple, capable of
being understood by anyone, independent of the past or
outside influences, and related to a period of time. Our
vision must be so clear and uncomplicated that a jogger
could shout the message out to casual listeners as he ran
through an area – and they would know exactly what the
vision was.

When our vision is this clearly defined, it gives us a cri-
terion by which we can assess everything we do. It helps
us to assess and measure our progress. When necessary,
it enables us to realign our activities.

### A vision which is distinctive

We need to take care that our vision is not dominated by
our location and our tradition or history – by where we
are and who we are. These are the starting points, not the
finishing line of growth!

Of course, appreciating where we stand in the
prophetic stream of church life can give us a sense of destiny. And understanding the social make-up of our area
can provide us with some ideas about how God intends
to use us. But our vision must be essentially independent
of these things.

The recent history of old churches can be oppressive,
because many negative attitudes are passed down along
with the positive aspects of our traditions. Too often,
people suggest, 'That is not our way'. If God is calling us
to do something new, we may have to change the way
that we work.

The greatest respect we can pay to our tradition and
history is to ensure that we do not contribute the full stop.
Instead, we should honour our tradition by making a distinct contribution which builds on the past's foundation.

## *A vision which is flexible*

It is also vital that our vision is not shaped by our buildings. If the building is not helpful, we should try to get
another one. Too much thinking about church growth is
governed and restricted by buildings.

When we are planting new churches in the London
City Church Network, we have very little to do with owning and maintaining buildings. I consider this to be one of
the greatest traps we can fall into. We prefer to hire public halls, community centres, schools, cinemas, libraries,
even public houses.

The leaders of one of our newest churches came to me
saying, 'We have found somewhere to meet.' 'Wonderful,'
I replied, 'We have been praying about this for a long
time.' They wanted to see my reaction when they told me
that it was in a pub! They were sure that they had the right
place because it was called 'The Lords' Bar'! These days,
more happens in the Lords' Bar than in the Public Bar
next door!

I can think of many situations where it would be
impossible or unhelpful to hold a church service in or
near a public bar, but this church's location has determined its character. It is on the edge of very great social
need and is now able to reach out to many people. A lot
of people have wandered in from the public bar, with
their drinks in their hands, to find out what is going on.
Some have found Jesus this way.

At times, we have been offered beautiful church buildings which other denominations have no longer wanted.
But the demographic changes in the area are the reason
why the building is empty. The buildings have been
impractical because not enough people live nearby to jus-
tify maintaining them.

We keep on having to ask ourselves, 'Is this building in
the right place?' 'Is it the right size for our present situation?' In London, it is often expensive and difficult to hire
halls; but this gives us more flexibility of vision and purpose than owning a building and having to maintain it.

However, there are advantages in owning or having exclusive use of a building. We need tremendous wisdom from God to ensure that we make the best use of our resources and do not allow them to control our decisions.

## *A vision which is targeted*

When we ask God to reveal his vision for our church, the single most important question we can put is: 'Whom are we meant to reach?' Our vision has to be shaped by the people whom we are called to reach with the gospel.

Most churches believe that they are called to try to reach *all* the people in their locality – rather than one particular group within the community.

This idea stems, in part, from the 'parish' system within the Church of England. But a bigger factor has been the confusion in thinking between New Testament local churches and modern local churches which we considered in chapter one.

Most recent expressions of the church have tried to be 'heterogeneous' units. This means that they have aimed to contain a balance of ages and social groups so that they accurately represent the social mixture in their area.

When a congregation thinks of itself as 'the local church', they are almost bound to believe that it is their responsibility to reach everyone in their locality.

This means that a church with – say – a thriving work among the elderly often feels bad about neglecting young people. Or a church with many white middle-class families is uncomfortable about the absence of black faces.

When congregations think about church growth they often focus on the sociological gaps in their midst. They target their weaknesses rather than their strengths – and, usually, try to reach them at the expense of their strengths!

This idea is based on a mistaken view of modern local churches as essentially independent units, and also on a wrong idea about unity.

Many leaders rightly think that the church should be some sort of counter-culture which prophetically shows the world how different social and ethnic groups can relate in love and trust. But they go on to assume that every expression of the church should evidence this para-culture unity solely 'within itself' rather than 'between themselves'.

The reality is that churches which aim to be heteroge-neous rarely succeed in reaching their goal. Despite what the minister may believe and maintain, the culture and style of the church will inevitably reflect the culture and style of the majority.

The leader may insist that the church is for everybody. They may speak a loud welcome before every opening hymn. But the unspoken message is, 'Come to us', 'Be like us', 'Dress like us', 'Worship like us', 'Speak like us'. People who are not comfortable with their culture and style will not feel welcome and will not be attracted. As a result, most allegedly heterogeneous churches are the clearest examples of homogenous churches around!

If they genuinely wanted to reach everybody, they would adapt their style of dress, culture, worship, preach-ing, thinking, hospitality, mission and so on. But, if they did that, they would probably lose many people from their own people group!

The heterogeneous model may seem good in theory, but it rarely works in practice and hardly ever facilitates cross-cultural growth.

Worship and witness are central to today's local churches. But different age groups, different social groups and different ethnic groups worship and witness in com-pletely different ways.

Worship which is culturally relevant and meaningful to elderly white middle-class believers is meaningless to young black working-class believers. The evangelistic methods which effectively reach Japanese students are useless at reaching Nigerian families – and so on.

A church which tries to reach every different group in a locality, and to do everything together in one congrega-tion, is likely either to reach nobody or to attract mainly one group.

In the London City Church Network, we have found

that church growth is facilitated when churches aim to be 'homogenous' units. This means recognising which 'people group' they have been called and equipped to reach, and then concentrating on making, maturing and mobilising disciples within that group. In practice, this means developing a special emphasis on a particular group rather than establishing an exclusive group.

As well as focusing on a particular people group, our community churches also concentrate on building 'unity in diversity' with the other expressions of the church in their locality and within the network.

In the network, we all come together regularly to celebrate, to train and learn, to develop our city church vision, and to express our unity in Jesus. We aim both for unity in our diversity and for diversity in our unity. We consider that we express our diversity by focusing on different people groups and show our unity by working together as part of an integrated whole.

Our vision at the central Kensington Temple congregation is mainly for young singles and ethnic minorities. We have developed a style of worship and a pattern of life which is relevant to these people groups. As a result, our services are packed out with Blacks, Asians and European students. Relatively few of our members are middle-class white families with young children.

However, we have established a large daughter church which mainly targets young white families – with a pattern of worship and witness that is relevant to them. Equally, we have also established churches which target the Chinese community – and dozens of other ethnic groups.

Each of our community churches has a clear vision of the people group that they are mainly trying to reach. However, each one also exists in a network of relationships which demonstrates the essential unity of the church.

Surprising though it may seem, it is precisely because we have based ourselves on the homogenous principle that our 'unity in diversity' is so incredibly enriching –

## Harvest Earl's Court

God first spoke to me about church planting when I was working with YWAM in India in 1984. I thought that he meant I would be involved in a new church – not that I would plant one myself!

In 1989, I was involved in street outreach in London. One day, whilst on the tube, God told me to get off the tube and go to Earl's Court because he wanted me to start work there.

I managed to get a room at the YWCA and began making contact with the local addicts, prostitutes and street people. As soon as this was known, I had to leave the YWCA. But a local Christian let me stay at her house, and I began a bible study there.

In the next few months, God gave me his heart of compassion for those involved in homosexuality, transexuality, prostitution and transvestism. I slowly realised that God was calling me to start a church for these people in the Earl's Court area.

I returned to the USA for two months to seek God's will. Was this really God's will or my own crazy idea? I came back to London certain that this was God's direction, but I had no idea how to start a church and there was nobody to help me.

Shortly after returning, God told me to write to Colin Dye at Kensington Temple, outlining the vision. I did this in October 1991, and was invited to meet him.

Apparently they had felt led to start a church

in Earl's Court, but the person they had asked to lead it had declined. Colin asked me how many people I wanted to help me start the work, but I told him that I thought God had called to start it from scratch.

I hired a room at the YWCA, and a small group met there weekly to prepare for a launch in February 1992. Our vision was to reach the street people. Within a few weeks of the launch, 20-25 people were coming – mainly from broken backgrounds. After three months, we were asked to leave the YWCA and had to meet at a local pub.

Because of all they had been through, the people who came were unstable and unreliable. I had to do everything myself. Sometimes it was unbearable and I cried to the Lord for help. Then God sent a believer with aids to my rescue, and he became a key leader.

Many Christians were interested in the work, but were afraid to be involved lest they be labelled as perverse – for we were known as a church full of people from perverse lifestyles. So I prayed for skilled workers. Gradually some came, and we began to grow. By 1995, about 50 people were regularly worshipping with us, and in January 1996 we appointed Yinka Adewole as pastor.

We now have four house-groups; have planted two other churches; and the early converts from various lifestyles are maturing and discipling other converts.

*Pastor Linda Patton*

especially when we meet together to celebrate. At the moment, over one hundred different national groups worship in Kensington Temple – and they all contribute out of the richness of their cultural backgrounds.

Personally, I feel that our regular worshipping and praying together is a clearer prophetic statement about the essential oneness of the body of Christ than in any so-called heterogeneous church. It is certainly louder!

I am sure that we could all do so much more, reach so many more people, if our churches had a clearer vision about whom they were trying to reach. One congregation will never reach everybody. Our style of worship and witness will largely determine whom we reach. If we stand with other churches, and trust them to reach other groups, the wider local church will grow.

Normally, we are best equipped to reach people of our own age and culture. Cross-cultural mission is difficult and demanding; tremendous sacrifices are needed to identify with a culture and assume its way of living. God does call many to reach a different cultural group – indeed much of the world can only be reached cross-culturally. But local congregations grow best by focusing on people like them.

Our unique holy vision begins when we identify those whom God is calling us to reach. It develops as we ask ourselves questions like, 'Where do the people in that group live?' 'What are they like?' 'How do they worship?' 'What is important to their culture? 'How can we learn about them?' 'How we can possibly reach them?'

Some churches rarely ask these questions. It is as if they open a shop and then wonder where the customers are. It is far too late when the shop is open. They should have put their shop where their customers are. Everything we do must be determined by the people we are trying to reach. They must be the basis of our vision.

## *A vision which is realistic*

No matter how clear we are about the people we are trying to reach, there must come a time when we stop acknowledging God's calling and start doing something about it.

A vision of a people group is not enough; we must anchor the vision in some God-inspired reality. Many churches are always praying about vision. They intercede and fast, but do little else. The heavenlies may shake with their shouting, yet little happens on earth.

Once we are clear about the people group we are targeting, we need God's answers to questions like 'How many?' and 'By when?'

Our vision at Kensington Temple is to become a fully functioning city church by the end of the decade – and to do this we think we need to be a network of 2,000 churches and groups. We believe that God gave us this vision through a mixture of prayer, discussion, realistic assessment of our situation, and an inspired off-the-cuff comment by a trusted and highly respected leader.

It is a big vision, but it is realistic. Why, if each of our churches planted one new church a year, we would have 3,000 churches by the end of the year 2,000!

Every church should have an easily identifiable vision which is both faith-stretching and utterly realistic. I find that this brings unity, releases energy, and provides people with a sense of purpose in their church life.

If a vision is to be realistic, it must be measurable – so that we can regularly evaluate our progress and take any steps necessary to get in line with the vision.

A realistic vision is also time-sensitive. Setting a vision within a time-scale is an important way of focusing attention. Once we start considering a vision in a specific time frame, we can see how our vision can become reality.

Too many so-called visions are really just dreams of good intentions. They remain vague until the leaders ask the how/what/when types of realistic questions.

I cannot provide anyone with a vision for their church. Instead, we all need to discover for ourselves God's vision for our situation. This is not a matter of human planning – though that does come into it. We need the Spirit to help us. We need his flash of inspiration. We need him to shape his vision as it gestates in us over a period of time.

We must look at where we are and at where God wants us to be. God's vision does not arrive on a piece of paper from heaven. Rather it is often something people identify with only after several months of prayer and discussion.

## REACHING OUR VISION

In the course of my work, I often travel to West Africa to visit a number of churches that we support and help. When a trip is coming up, I know that I have to travel a huge distance from my home in London.

We can say that my vision is to reach an African city on a particular date. The vision is clear, realistic and time-related. But it is impossible for me to get from where I am to where I want to be in one step. I need to break the journey down into defined, manageable and executable steps. I call this developing strategies.

### *Develop our strategies*

Strategies are the steps we need to take to reach a vision. It is amazing what becomes possible when we break a vision down into these small steps.

There is an old joke which asks, 'How do you eat an elephant?' The answer is, 'One bite at a time.' If we piled into a room everything that the average person eats in a year, it would be a surprising amount. If we gave it to someone, and told them to eat it, they would be horrified. But it would seem easy if we said, 'Eat this, by eating one plateful, three times a day, for a year'. This is developing a strategy to reach a vision.

By strategies, a great big vision can be broken down into manageable units. But we do have to be committed to the vision or we will not bother to break it into units. As in all things to do with God, it takes persistence to get through.

For example, the Bible contains sixty six books and 1,189 chapters. A new believer would stumble if we gave them a Bible and told them to read from Genesis to Revelation in one go. However, it would be a realistic vision if we asked them to read it through in one year.

A strategy we could develop to help them reach this vision would be to suggest that they read two chapters in the morning and two chapters in the evening for six days a week. If they started on January 1st, they would reach the end of Revelation by mid December.

As I have said, our vision is to be a fully-functioning city church by the end of the decade, and we think that we need to establish 2,000 groups and churches to be this.

To help us reach this vision, we have had to develop strategies for training leaders, strategies for determining localities and people groups which need churches, and strategies for nurturing the new churches. We know that these strategies have to be in place if we are to reach our vision in God's time-span.

## Mobilise our resources

If we are going to reach a worthwhile vision, it will cost us something. We will need resources. In Luke 14:28-32 Jesus made it plain that we should never start something without checking that we can complete it.

I have found that God does not give us all the resources for the whole task at the beginning. But he does give us everything we need to start, and he does provide us with what we need as we go along. As we have prayed and interceded, so God has sent people who are exactly the resource we need to help at a certain time.

We must work hard at discovering and releasing our resources. This begins by appreciating and explaining that all resources are wrapped up in people.

For example, we might think that we need £100 to buy some chairs, when what we really need is for someone to give the £100 or the chairs. Or we might think that we need to hire a hall, when we really need someone to find the right hall and someone to agree to let it to us. Resources always come down to people, and we need to pray, think and plan accordingly.

Then we must make our people aware of the resources we need. We do this by encouraging them to pray in 'people-centred language'. Surely this is why Jesus told us in Luke 10:2 to pray for the Lord of the harvest to send labourers: these were the key resources for reaping – not cut-price sickles and second-hand scythes.

The strange fact is that, when people start praying for resources in this way, they soon want to do the job themselves. They want to become the resources for which they are praying.

At Kensington Temple, whenever we have a need we arrange a prayer meeting. I might pray, 'Lord, we need a piano and someone to play it in the latest church that we are planting'.

There may be three people in the prayer meeting who can play the piano and another three who own pianos. At first, they respond by praying, 'Lord, send someone who owns a piano, and send someone who can play the piano'. Then the Spirit reminds them, 'Hey! You have a piano you never use', and 'Come on! You've got Grade Eight – you could play for them'. Soon some of them will be saying, 'Here am I, Lord, send me; use my talent; use my piano'.

Resources are vital, but if we do not mobilise the people to provide or to be the resources, the vision will not be reached.

### Implement our strategies

The strategies must be set in motion, step by step. It is vitally important that this is done at a leadership level in the church. Leaders must manage the strategies and supervise their implementation.

I know this sounds like the language of a business-school, but it is simply a modern application of the New Testament teaching about the functions of deacons and elders, the diversity of ministries, and so on.

A strategy will not be effective unless someone is responsible for it – and that should be the person who is gifted to manage it.

Some churches make the mistake of assuming that the person who receives God's vision for a strategy should be the person to implement it. That is not necessarily true. Some people are gifted in original thinking but useless at managing projects – they are different skills.

Other churches expect the minister or the elders to manage all the strategies. Again, that is not necessarily best. It depends on people's giftings. However, there must be a significant leader in the church who is responsible for each significant strategy. There should be a leader over every strategy with the sole responsibility of managing the strategy and of reporting regularly to the corporate leadership.

This might seem rather remote and idealistic in a small church. But it is important to learn the skills of teamwork and delegation right at the start. Leaders who can delegate 'the getting the room right' strategy when there are only twenty people, will not burden themselves unnecessarily when that strategy has grown to 'hiring an auditorium, lights and P.A.'.

I know that it is harder to delegate, involve others, recognise different ministries, and so on, when a church is small. We all think that we can do the job better than anyone else. But I promise that small churches grow faster when the leader gives real responsibility to others.

This is partly because the leaders can spend more time praying and preparing their sermons. It is also partly because other people are attracted to situations where they feel useful and know that they can make a real contribution. More importantly, it is also because 'team ministry' is God's pattern for his church. Few things have stifled growth more than the 'one man ministry' idea – this has paralysed too many churches for far too long.

## Review our strategies

I believe that there should be regular reviews in every area of strategy: annual, quarterly, monthly, even weekly where necessary.

At Kensington Temple, we have a quarterly board

## The Chiswick Christian Centre

In the mid 1990s, I was a KT staff worker when the 'Toronto Blessing' was strongest. God challenged me through this to respond to him in a new way. I was head of Pastoral Ministries, but felt a strong urge to get out and spread the gospel; and I knew that church planting was the most effective means.

In early 1995, we were discussing potential areas for church plants. It was mentioned that many of our members lived in Chiswick, and I investigated starting something there. A building became available, then it fell though, and plans were shelved.

Another building became available in January 1996. Our proposal was accepted in April and we moved in at the start of May. I presented the plans in April and May, and 52 members of the main congregation signed six month commitment forms.

Prayer meetings were held in the Chiswick building throughout May, and leaflets were distributed in the surrounding area.

110 adults and 25 children attended the first service on Pentecost Sunday 1996. In the next week we hosted the evangelistic play *'Heaven's gates and hell's flames'*. 350 people came to see this: 80 responded to the gospel, 60 of them for the first time.

Among our early challenges was the problem of chairs. The building did not have any! We managed to find 250 ex hotel chairs, but needed to raise £2,500 to pay for them.

An Indonesian business man was in London for two days. He looked for a church in the phone book, and walked into a service literally as I was appealing for people to sponsor a chair. He gave all the cash he had – £1000 – and the chairs were paid for almost immediately.

After six months, 100 adults had some level of commitment to the new church. Most Sundays, there were about 70 adults and 15 children at the service. Each week, we saw one or two people make a commitment to Christ in the services – and most of these stayed with the church.

We ran an Alpha course right from the start, and this greatly helped the early converts. We also established a fortnightly club for retired people, a weekly Youth Club, and a weekly Parents and Toddlers group which attracts 50 parents. Our main evangelistic strategy is distributing copies of the Jesus film on video to homes in the locality.

Most of the 52 people from KT stayed on after their six month commitment. A large part of the success is down to their sacrifice of time and money.

At first I worked part-time, but I became full time and fully financed after four months. We expect to continue to grow in the future.

*Pastor Gareth Lewis*

meeting when major reports are submitted on every strategy. The purpose of this is to compare our progress with our vision. I find it amazing how, just a few months into the year, people forget the direction and time-scale. Instead of running the church, we let the church run us!

We must avoid directionless church life. We must not allow meetings merely to happen so that several months pass and we have not moved a step closer to the vision.

Reviews are important times. They show us where there are obstacles and missing resources. They are times for creative problem solving and adjusting strategies. The vision does not change, but we often have to refine the steps towards that vision.

Reviews help us to apply the wisdom we have gained from our experience in the strategy. By doing this, we are now planting better churches than before. And we are planting them quicker, with greater understanding.

## Press on to the vision

We need to focus all our energy on reaching the vision. If we know where we are going, and how to get there, we should get on with the journey. We must stop wasting time on other distractions!

There are many things which seem to be good for a church to do, but we must not let the good be the enemy of the best. The devil is more likely to prevent our church from growing by distracting us with worthy causes than by confronting us with a major obstacle.

His best is the only thing that God wants us to do. People will suggest many activities which seem to be good works for churches to perform, but we must come back and insist that this is not our primary vision.

If we pursue strategies or activities which are not our central focus we will dissipate our energies. Instead, we should harness all our efforts together as a congregation to achieve what Jesus is specifically calling us to do.

God will not give us a vision which we cannot reach. But we are unlikely to reach the vision without total commitment and tightly focused attention.

# QUESTIONS

1. What social, age and ethnic groups mainly make up your church?

2. Which group of people are you aiming to reach? How could you reach them more effectively?

3. What, precisely, is God's vision for your church? How was this decided upon?

4. How would the average member of your church answer Question Three?

5. What strategies are in place for reaching the vision? How have these been developed in the last three years?

6. If there is no clear vision, what action do you need to take to establish God's vision for your church?

7. If there is a vision but no strategies, what action do you need to take to establish effective strategies?

8. How could your strategies be better managed and reviewed?

## *FOUR*

# Getting the details right

Some leaders have wonderful vision. They can even see the strategies which are needed to reach that vision. But they flounder around never reaching their destiny because they do not attend to the small details.

Equally, other leaders are masters of detail. Everything is highly organised and business-like. But they do not know where they are going or where God wants them to go.

Church leaders need to be both effective and efficient. We need to do the right thing and we need to do things right. We must ensure that we have God's vision clearly in focus and that we attend to all the relevant small details.

1 Kings 18 is a wonderful illustration of how vision plus details equal growth. Elijah knew that God's agenda for the people of Israel was to turn away from Baal and return to Yahweh. His strategy was a confrontation on Carmel. Verses 30-35 show how he attended to the tiny details. Verse 39 reports the magnificent result.

## BEHIND THE SCENES

I believe that creative, detailed planning is one of the primary responsibilities of management. Growth can only happen when we dedicate themselves to this task – or when we delegate it to those who are gifted in this area. But we must ensure that planning involves praying to the Father, asking him for wisdom and guidance, before we plan together how we can implement what God has shown us.

## Structures for growth

A church will often reach a certain peak of growth and then level off. This commonly happens after a particular strategy or project has been completed.

In the mid 80's, we needed a significant breakthrough at Kensington Temple. We realised that we had outgrown the way we organised the church and needed to change our basic leadership structure.

We appointed several leaders to head up four divisions, with various departments and activities grouped together in each division. Our divisions were evangelism, training, pastoral care, and administration. Since then, we have needed to add five more divisions – church planting, finance, social ministries, communications and music.

This may seem a logical business-like decision, but we cannot run a church in the same way as a business. Of course, there should be a sound business structure; but we have got to hear from God in these matters.

We took several days over the process. We met together outside of our normal setting to create an unpressurised environment for planning. We prayed and laughed together. We submitted our ideas and suggestions. We talked until we found we had something that we believed was from God. We had to work at it, but eventually we found a structure which seemed good to the Spirit and us.

Through this experience, we learned how important it is for leaders to meet outside the normal church environment in a place where they can be free to think new thoughts and plan creatively.

Of course, we do not need to wait for a plateau to structure for growth. It is much better if we prepare for growth by adjusting our structures to accommodate the expected growth. This is what we do in our 'natural' lives.

I remember when my wife and I were expecting our first child. There was one room in our house which was my pride and joy. It was my study, which was filled with my beloved books and files. But suddenly I was out because the baby was coming!

I did not think of this as a sacrifice: it was a pleasure to make room for our new baby. In fact, I personally decorated the room: there was new wallpaper, new curtains, new carpet and quite different furniture. We were planning for growth so we were changing our structures to prepare for the anticipated growth!

If only the same attitude prevailed in our churches. We must plan for growth. Too much time is taken up with ensuring that 'we' are comfortable and that 'we' have what we want.

A close and tight knit church can become what sociologists call a 'primary group'. It has its own history and ethos, and is difficult to join. The members know each other well, get together after the meetings, and newcomers feel left out. For many people, the time for 'fellowship and coffee' after the service is the loneliest and most unwelcoming part of church life. This is particularly acute in smaller churches.

This problem will be solved only when members work together to plan for growth and to focus their attention outwards. We need times when the whole church brainstorms and asks questions like: 'What steps are necessary to reach people outside the church?' 'How can we release people to evangelise?' 'What are the features of our church which attract people?' 'What are the features of our church that do not attract people?' 'How can we deal with one and enhance the other?'

Once we have addressed these issues, and thought creatively about them, we can begin to plan for growth and to put the details into place.

Some churches are cutting down the number of their services. Instead of attending the usual weekly round of services, the members are urged to go out and make contacts, to invite people for hospitality, to get involved in positive social events to build relationships. They see this equally as being part of 'service'.

Although we are not closing any services at Kensington Temple, we are helping our people to reach out. Who says that a church service must be held in a church building? Where is the verse which insists that a service is primarily Christians meeting to listen to a sermon? Too much happens in church life only because it has always happened. But who stops to ask whether it helps the church to grow?

Every church should decide whether the existing structures of meetings, activities and organisation are helping or hindering growth. We need to decide for ourselves what God is saying about structuring for growth, and then have the courage to change whatever needs to be changed. We must plan and prepare for babies.

### Mobilise the people

If we compare the New Testament church with today's church, one of the most noticeable differences is that the real work of ministry was carried out by the members. In the early church, the leaders released the people to do the work of Christ. Today, the people usually pay the minister to do it – and the minister accepts the role without question.

We must get back to the New Testament practice. It was the believers who evangelised. They reached out to their friends. They used their homes for fellowship, breaking bread and building each other up. We, however, have brought everyone into a building and called it 'church'.

We are plagued by two false ideas. We do not understand leadership and we do not understand membership. Leadership is given by God to release and equip the membership; and the membership is given by God to do the work of Jesus Christ.

Some leaders give their people this impression, 'Of course you all have a ministry. Your ministry is to listen to me. Occasionally you can arrange the flowers, gather the hymn books, work the over-head projector and make the coffee. But, basically, God is happy as long as you're here each Sunday.'

The whole church on earth is Christ's body on earth, which means that Jesus' will and ministry must be done through his whole body. If all the members are not mobilised and released, the work of God will not be done. No clever and frenetic activity by ministers can ever compensate for that. Our churches will not grow beyond a certain point if a few gifted people do all the work. They will only multiply if all God's people work in his gifting and power.

This radical transformation is not easy in old churches, where the believers believe that the minister is meant to do everything. However, people can be mobilised by a mixture of prayer, teaching and detailed planning.

It is up to those of us who are ministers. We *can* delegate. We *can* involve others. We *can* train and release people. We often think it will be quicker if we carry out a task ourselves. It may be at first, but such an attitude prevents growth. We will plan and carry out the mass mobilisation of our members only when we recognise that our primary calling and responsibility is to equip the saints for the work of ministry.

All the time leaders think that they should take all the meetings, run all the marriage preparation classes, make all the pastoral visits, follow up all the visitors, and so on, they will not be performing their most important task. Good works will have distracted them from God's best. Their so-called ministerial activity will be an obstacle to church growth.

Mobilisation is not only about exhortation. Mobilisation also requires detailed planning. People need to be given specific, purposeful jobs to do. They need to be trained and supervised in their tasks. They need to be assessed, corrected, encouraged, and given greater tasks and responsibilities. It is no good giving someone a task and then leaving them to flounder: there must be planning and partnership.

I guarantee that you will see people flourish as you release them in ministry. The work of God will multiply and the church of Christ will grow.

## BUILDINGS

Every church has to meet somewhere. It may be a home, a hired hall or a building we own which has been a place of worship for centuries. If a church is to grow, it must think about where it meets and make sure that all the necessary details are planned correctly.

As a church grows, it will often need to change the format in the building. For example, straight rows of seats are usually inappropriate for congregations of under forty and a congregation of eighty should not sit in a circle!

Sooner or later, every growing church has either to change its building or to find new buildings for its freshly planted daughter churches.

### *Buildings must be accessible*

Some traditional church buildings are no longer accessible to the general public, especially in cities where buildings are being torn down and bus routes diverted. If people cannot get to a building easily – or if they do not know where it is – they will not come.

This may not be an issue if our building is well established in the community. Even so, we need to ensure that our building is not accessible only to those who own cars. If it is, we will be excluding the elderly and the poor.

When we plant new churches in the London City Church Network, we face the twin problems of accessibility and visibility. We have to grapple with issues like transport and parking. We must ensure that the building is clearly sign-posted and that the entrance is well marked – these may need delicate negotiations with unsympathetic authorities.

If we go into a public building, we do not want to go

up and down in the lift trying to find the person we want
to see. In a department store or shopping precinct, we
need a good plan so that we know where to do our shopping. Church planning needs to be this practical and
detailed.

For example, one of our churches met for a time in the
local swimming bath. The entrance to the meeting hall
was deep inside the building – you had to go through corridor after corridor to find it. In order for this to work
there had to be clear signs directing people with a series
of arrows – it also helped to have smiling stewards to
direct the people and reassure them that they were on the
right track.

Churches which are growing find ways to ensure that
their buildings are accessible and that people can find
their way there easily. Many provide newcomers with
maps so that they can find the homes of the leaders and
home-groups without any difficulty. If we are serious
about growth, we will do everything possible to ensure
that people cannot miss where we are meeting.

Most people associate 'church' with a particular type of
building, but new churches usually have to meet in
schools, community halls, hotel rooms, and so on. We
need to avoid looking like a strange sect and ensure that
our directional signs clearly identify us as a bona fide
Christian group.

### Buildings must be comfortable

It is obvious that our building should be well heated in
winter and well ventilated in summer. It should be well lit,
with appropriate seating and all unnecessary distractions
removed. People like to go somewhere nice, so every
effort must be made to make the room attractive.

Although these things seem absolutely basic, they may
be beyond some new churches. Sometimes the only
available hall will not be properly lit; it may have inappropriate seating and many other disadvantages. When we
are faced with a difficult choice, we need to remember

that a dreadful hall in a great location is better than a wonderful hall in the middle of nowhere.

I was recently part of a church planting programme in Cambridgeshire. The new church was going to meet in a local cinema which was on two levels: downstairs was set out like a restaurant, and upstairs was a conventional auditorium.

The snag was that the people upstairs could see the screen but not the platform below and the seats in the restaurant were attached to the tables! This meant that I had people who could see a blank screen but not me, and people who were sitting round tables trying to turn and look. These are some of the obstacles we have to overcome when planting new churches!

Some leaders tell me that they do not have a problem because their church building is well established. I always ask them to take a look at their buildings from an outsider's point of view. Is it attractive and welcoming? Is it clean and comfortable? Can people see and hear what goes on?

Many churches use OHP screens which are illegible to the people at the back and the elderly, and to everyone on a sunny day! Or they have so many books and leaflets that outsiders never know what page they are meant to be on.

I once pastored a church which looked like a graveyard. The brickwork was incredibly dark and depressing, but the people who had built it thought it was Buckingham Palace! At my first church business meeting, I asked how we could make the building more attractive. When I opened my mouth I realised that I had made a serious error!

But gradually the people began to see how unwelcoming the building was. There was no lighting on the outside and – to conserve heat – instead of opening the front doors they used a little side entrance. The people who regularly worshipped there did not mind: they knew how to get in. But nobody driving past would have dreamt that anything good ever happened there.

## Putney Christian Fellowship

In September 1995, it seemed to me that the Lord spoke to me clearly, telling me that he wanted me to plant churches in South West London through the London City Church Network.

I was sure that God was prompting me to start in Putney, and that the church should be a 'church planting church'.

I started 'work' on the vision at the beginning of 1996 – gathering information; gauging the spiritual climate; trying to understand the social, cultural and racial context; and praying for the area.

I tried to gather together the KT people who lived in the area, but only four of the 35 people shared the vision. I spent many long hours praying for people to share the vision which God had given me.

I felt my main task was to pass on the vision for Putney and motivate people. Despite many frustrations, people gradually came forward. Many of us started to believe the impossible and see beyond our small numbers and difficult circumstances.

In May we went 'public' and organised a very successful *Alpha* course. By early June 1996, there were 10 people who had known each other for only a few weeks. We prayed and shared together, expecting to launch at the end of the year.

Then, suddenly, we were asked to become a

pioneer satellite-broadcast centre – which meant launching that July! Under this scheme, a monthly or weekly KT service is broadcast live by satellite to help new church plants become established and to feel an integral part of the LCC Network.

A week before the July launch, we still had no musicians or children's workers, yet – amazingly – 65 people turned up at the launch and 45 people attended the next service.

After that, God blessed us in an incredible way. Within three months of starting, 60 people were regularly attending and we had excellent worship and children's ministry teams.

When God envisioned us, I was sure that the church should reflect Putney's multi-national nature and plant other churches. Within six months, 15 nations were represented and a group were meeting to prepare for a new church in Wimbledon.

We have since held another *Alpha* course, and have developed a new course *Journey into Light* to help us reach the many 'New Agers' in the area.

There is much to be done, so we are building strong relationships with other local churches through prayer meetings and shared activities. We know the battle will be hard, but we are convinced that what God has promised will come to pass.

*Pastor Alex Tana*

These tiny details matter. If we want our church to grow, we will try to see how we appear to people in the locality – and take steps to rectify any problems.

The size of the room is also important. If it is too small the meeting will be cramped and uncomfortable. If it is too big it will seem unwelcoming and there will be a sense of failure.

One church I was involved in helping plant got off the ground with a good launch. Many more people than expected attended the first few meetings, and over 50 people were crammed into a room for 30.

There was another room available in the same complex which seated 250 people, and the leaders were convinced that we should move into this room. They felt that this was a step of faith. Actually, it was rather foolish.

There were many people who came at first 'to see what it was like' but had no intention of getting involved. The numbers quickly dropped to 35 – and this coincided with the move to the larger room. We had 35 people in a room for 250 and the dynamics of the meetings changed instantly.

Instead of it being a successful meeting with people excitedly crammed in, it had a sense of failure as people rattled around in a huge room. This new church had to learn its lessons the hard way!

## MEETINGS

If we want our churches to grow, we will also need to take care of all the details in our meetings. In recent years, some leaders have over-stressed the place of spontaneity. They seem to think that being inspired by the Spirit ten seconds before speaking is superior to being inspired ten days before the meeting!

Personally, I believe that we need thoroughly to prepare every aspect of our meetings, trusting the Spirit to inspire us well in advance. We need to intercede for God's guidance and blessing for a meeting well beforehand. On their own, last minute vestry prayers are simply not adequate. Of course, we should always be ready to adjust our plans at the last minute if it is plain that God has something different for us to do or say.

### Sensible welcomes

Churches which are growing always have a good welcome for visitors. Newcomers are quickly made to feel at ease. They are neither ignored nor overpowered.

In Britain, newcomers do not like to be identified in an embarrassing way. If we asked our visitors to stand up many of them would probably never come back! Yet, in some parts of the world, people would not feel welcomed unless they were greeted in a highly visible manner. We need considerable cultural sensitivity in welcoming people.

This is a key area where some members of the congregation should have special responsibility for greeting visitors and helping them to feel comfortable.

We should all ask ourselves how we identify newcomers and make them feel at home. At Kensington Temple we give them a welcome booklet. At some stage in every meeting, one of the leaders says something like this: 'Now, for those who are newcomers today, we would like to welcome you by giving this booklet. In it you can find out who we are as a church, what we believe, and what we are trying to do. In the middle section, you will see something that we have written with you in mind – that is, if you're not familiar with our form of worship. We explain why we worship as we do. Basically it's all about getting excited about Jesus. We think that it's OK to get excited about him!'

Then we say, 'Inside there's a form that we'd really like you to fill in as your way of introducing yourself to us. Please complete it during the meeting and hand it to a steward at the end of the service. There will be people to welcome you and give you a cup of tea or coffee and answer any questions you may have.'

While the leader is speaking, stewards walk round with a pile of booklets and a smile; we find that most visitors naturally indicate with a small gesture if they want a booklet.

This has been a great aid, and we now give out over 10,000 copies each year to newcomers. It is a colourful booklet which clearly identifies people as visitors. If anyone is carrying one, our members know that this is someone to greet especially warmly.

In smaller churches, it is much easier to identify a newcomer. Even so, it is helpful to have something to give them which lets them know what is happening. I think it is vital for a church to have some simple means of sensitively obtaining every newcomer's name and address – so that they can be visited or contacted within forty-eight hours.

### Time of meeting

Our meetings need to be held at the most suitable time for the people we are seeking to reach. Most British Christians associate church services with Sunday morning at eleven, but there may be good reasons for holding our main service at a substantially different time.

Meetings must not start late, contain too many items, and take too long. In many churches, there is a tendency for the sermons and worship to be too long and so be off-putting to newcomers.

Most visitors are comfortable with a sixty minute service, and this should contain worship, preaching and ministry in roughly equal proportions. While there are no hard and fast rules, it is far better to have one good hour of quality, planned service – which leaves people wanting more – than two hours of an unstructured free-for-all which people find exhausting or tedious.

### Holy worship

Worship is critical to church growth. We need lively, joyful, varied worship with skilful music. We need to offer God the best that we can from our culture and tradition.

The worship style must be appropriate to the size of the venue and culturally relevant to the people who attend. Some leaders have seen our massive PA system at Kensington Temple and the flamboyant way that our meetings are led. Foolishly, they have then tried to transfer the same PA system and worship style to a building which seats twenty five people!

I am astonished at how some leaders insist on using platforms in small buildings, and try to lead tiny congregations as if they were huge celebrations. It is as if they do not feel that they are preaching unless they are standing behind a pulpit. When there is a congregation of twenty-five people or less, it is usually better to sit in a circle and lead from a chair – preaching with a Bible in the lap.

The style and culture of a meeting should always be inclusive. This is true even when we are targeting a particular cultural group. Some churches seem to put their culture before Christ and are in danger of becoming too narrow in focus. Often, all that is needed is a simple explanation which draws people into a shared experience of a different style or culture.

Where the church uses a foreign language, it is necessary to show an awareness of people outside that language group. For example, providing simultaneous translation is often an aid to growth.

Of course, we do not need to speak a foreign language to appear foreign to outsiders. Most services contain too much jargon and too many phrases which are incomprehensible – or just plain silly – to those outside the faith. We must make every effort to make our language clear, accessible and sensible to newcomers.

The music in meetings is bound to reflect our ethnic and cultural preferences, but our personal taste must not dominate. There is always a place for 'church' music, as newcomers will feel more comfortable if there are some hymns and styles which they know from their childhood – or even from Songs of Praise! The traditional base of organ or piano can be augmented with other styles and instruments as appropriate.

Most LCC congregations use a charismatic or Pentecostal style of worship, yet much that passes for modern charismatic worship is not the real thing. Spirit-directed worship is not a style of doing things it is an openness to the Spirit and his gifts within any style!

Every church needs to think through for themselves what Spirit-filled worship means for them. A church which is truly directed by the Spirit in its worship will be fresh rather than stale and predictable.

Whatever style is used, we need constantly to explain our distinctives to newcomers. For example, the raising of hands, praying in tongues and shouting 'Hallelujah' can be culturally alienating. Yet a simple, brief explanation can break down these barriers.

The presence of God is the most important thing that we can have in our services. This is not a question of size or resources. God's presence is available to everybody – whether we are leading the worship with a single guitar, an old-fashioned organ or an eight-piece band. Any additions, as important as they may be in their own way, are no substitute for God's presence.

An unbeliever can walk into a room that is cold, bare, badly equipped, and be touched by the presence of God. It is not because these things do not matter, it is merely that we can have beautiful carpets, superb equipment and be without God's power.

People are unlikely to join the church if we have not prayed down God's presence. Even if they do, they are likely to be 'club members' rather than partners with the Holy Spirit.

It is the spiritual disciplines of prayer, fasting, meditating, waiting and wrestling with God which bring God's presence to our meetings and worship. Please do not forget these details. Never think that you can get by without them.

I know one pastor who was reading the Didache – a second century book of the church. He felt that God was going to show him the secret of power. Personally, I think that he should have stuck with the book of Acts, but he went to this extra piece of writing and found a section about fasting.

The book looks at Jesus' words, 'Do not fast like the hypocrites', and asks, 'How do they fast?' Well, they fasted on Tuesdays and Thursdays, so the early church said, 'We will fast on Wednesdays and Fridays,' and completely missed the point of what Jesus was saying. Yet my pastor friend followed the book and started to fast every Wednesday and Friday. The moment that he did, his church started to grow!

Please do not copy him. There are no slick techniques for bringing down the presence of God into our lives and into our meetings. God simply wants us to be serious about him – and to prove it by our actions.

It is not what my friend did that matters, it is that he showed how serious he was about God's presence. We all need to get alone with him and to go on seeking his face until we breakthrough in this area.

## Formal informality

I believe that we need to create a relaxed atmosphere in our meetings, but that the whole church must be well structured. Everything in the meeting – the prayers, the notices, the offering, the readings and so on – must be performed with excellence but without a clinical perfection.

At first, when people started leading the churches we had planted, they were too informal in their approach. There was hardly any structure to the meetings. The leaders had misread my relaxed presentation, the way the service flowed, and the way that people felt comfortable in the services. They did not see the intense preparation and the sophisticated pattern below the surface.

It is rather like those evenings when visitors come to our homes for a meal. We keep all the hard work out of sight. Five minutes before the visitors arrive, one partner says, 'They'll be here in a minute,' and there is a mad rush to get everything ready in time. But when the doorbell rings, we suddenly become quite calm and collected. 'Oh hallo, welcome, how nice to see you,' one of us says –

while the other one is frantically shooing the children upstairs!

We do the entertaining and, by the end of the evening, the kitchen looks like World War Three. The visitors say, 'Can we help you with anything?' 'Of course not,' we all reply, and then spend two hours cleaning up after they have left!

We keep the preparation and tidying up from them because we are the hosts and they are the guests. We want them to relax and enjoy themselves. Church services are much the same. We have to make sure that the people – especially newcomers – can relax and receive from God. But hours, days even, of prayer and hard work must go into preparing the structure and detailed content of the meeting.

### Relevant sermons

In growing churches, the sermons will be clear, relevant, simple, beneficial, and not too long! We need to ask ourselves what the people need to hear, what is God's word for this week.

We should learn from Jesus. He pointed to the flowers and talked about things which were relevant to the people in an agricultural society. We need to be equally relevant to our age and culture.

Sadly, it seems to me that the art of sermon preparation – the craft of shaping a talk – is a dying skill. The standard of preaching seems to be deteriorating rapidly. But it need not be this way, as long as leaders are prepared to learn and to work hard at their preparation.

Too many leaders trust the Spirit to inspire them when they stand up on their feet. They should have been pleading with him to inspire them days before the meeting when they were studying.

It is the leader's responsibility to make sure that the sermons are preached from scripture and are relevant and applicable to everyday lives. A preacher can spout long, deep sermons, peppered with Greek and Hebrew words, but they are useless unless they impact ordinary lives.

Some sermons lack substance. Others do not feed people. Still more are cold and never produce laughter or tears. I think that preachers should ask themselves these sort of challenging questions: 'Does this message make sense to my listeners?' 'Will people remember this message after the service?' 'Do I keep people's attention throughout the talk?' 'Is there enough information for it to be applied in everyday life?' 'How will people use the message?' 'How can I touch their emotions?' 'How can I move their wills?'

We must all be challenged to communicate effectively. At the very least, we should record our messages and listen to them later so that we can constructively criticise ourselves.

No matter how good the content, congregations switch off when preachers fails to present their messages in a way which grasps their listeners' attention. Too many preachers listen at a conference to a gifted communicator then go home and preach a talk of the same length. Yet they cannot maintain their congregation's attention for that length of time.

Somehow, we must find ways of creatively teaching God's word in a way which meets the needs of today's generation. We need to learn from modern media and communication skills, yet ensure that all our teaching is centred on Christ. A list of do's and don'ts helps nobody, people need to know Jesus and the life we find only in him.

Once, when I first started out, a man came to me after one particular sermon and said, 'When are you going to illustrate your sermons?' 'From now on,' I replied, 'Beginning with you!' Every time I give a talk about preaching now, I use him as an illustration!

Some of us have to learn the hard way. It was difficult for me as, by an immature conviction, I would not read a book about learning to preach. I naïvely believed that it was unspiritual to try and learn how to preach. I thought that I should pray, seek God for a message, and then give it.

## Riverside Community Church

I was saved in 1982 while I was at university in Ghana studying fine art. I then came to England for post-graduate studies – hoping that my training in arts would help me communicate the gospel.

In 1989, I took a year out to study at the International Bible Institute of London, fully expecting to return to computer graphics at the end of the year.

During the second term, I felt called by God to full-time ministry; and at the end of the year I was invited by the KT elders to join their one year pastoral apprenticeship scheme. As part of this, I worked with a fellow apprentice in a church plant in Kilburn.

At the end of that year, I was assigned to help plant a satellite church in Palmers Green – we decided to call it the Riverside Community Church.

Our first service was held in May 1991 in an empty church building which we agreed to rent – we still use it today. 15 adults attended that first service – and all of them were from KT.

None of the core group lived in Palmers Green, they had simply committed themselves to travelling in on a Sunday for six months to support the services and help establish the work as best they could.

In the first year, my wife and I distributed leaflets in the area which introduced what we were trying to do.

We held barbecues and gave out tracts in the local park. We conducted a survey of the community, and this really helped us introduce ourselves to the neighbourhood.

During the first twelve months, numbers climbed from 12 to 25 adults at each service. But this fell back to 12 by the time all the core group had returned to KT.

Before the first year was up, in February 1992, I became responsible for the church. I worked part time for the next four years as a caretaker until the church reached a position where it could support me full-time in the ministry. Through all this time, I was greatly helped by the training, support and oversight of Kensington Temple and other LCC congregations.

Our church growth has been slow but constant. We have not had a great mass of conversions; instead we have seen an average of one person coming to the Lord in most months.

We grew from 12 to 30 adults by 1994, and then to 60 by 1996. By the end of 1996, there were about 80 adults with some level of commitment to the church.

We currently have three cell groups, and these will soon develop into churches. Our vision is to develop, as part of the London City Church, a network of linked churches throughout this part of London. We are well on the way to seeing that take shape.

*Pastor Bediako Bosque-Hamilton*

I had made a whole heap of false assumptions. Sermons must have shape, colour, texture, pace and variety. They must grip people, take them on a journey, show them where they are going, and deliver them safely at the destination.

One of the hardest skills for me to learn was ending a sermon. Now I always plan exactly how I am going to finish – so that I do not keep flying and miss the runway! We must have all seen preachers do this. We think that they are coming in to land. They line up their approach, and we begin to fasten our seat belts. What a relief, we are coming home! Then, suddenly, just when the preacher should be easing off the throttle, he suddenly remembers another point and takes off again!

Some preachers never learn to land the plane. They suddenly stop short and that is it. We are left feeling jolted from the suddenness of the stop, like a passenger in a plane which has crash-landed.

## WIDER CHURCH LIFE

In many ways, it is easy to ensure that we attend to all the details about buildings and meetings. It is obvious when we have a problem with these areas. Growing churches, however, do not stop there. They ensure that they attend to all the details in every area of their church life.

### Efficient administration

Growing churches are efficiently administered. People often judge a church by the standards of its administration. They are unlikely to be attracted if they get a scribbled note from the Pastor in a scrappy envelope.

We must pay attention even to simple things like replying to letters promptly and politely, and treating people courteously on the telephone. If a meeting is cancelled, we must make sure that everyone knows. This type of careful administration shows how much we value the people who attend or are likely to attend. If people feel valued, it is more probable that they will return.

## *Quality relationships*

Growing churches build quality relationships by having a variety of activities. There is a real need for people to have contact with each other outside the main services. It simply is not good enough to shake hands with someone after the service and say, 'Hallo, how are you? God bless you; see you next week.'

When there are no opportunities to establish relationships, people sag spiritually in the middle of the week. They attend a church service to get propped up for a few more days. Churches which do not meet the most basic human needs of friendship and fellowship simply do not grow.

Whatever the size of our congregation, we must provide a variety of opportunities for people to build relationships. The mid-week house-group type of meeting is often not that attractive to men. Women tend to be comfortable meeting in homes – they visit them naturally as they raise their children. Whereas most men rarely visit homes: they tend to be more comfortable in a pub, hotel room or sporting venue.

Growing churches have small groups, house groups, goal-directed activities, sporting activities, special interest groups – a whole host of opportunities for meaningful interaction.

Obviously, smaller churches cannot provide all these activities at the same time, but they can vary what they do through the year. Some people like to meet at a home bible study. Others prefer to decorate an elderly member's lounge. A few might play tennis together in the summer.

If we want our church to grow, we will ensure that we are helping people to build quality relationships which are not exclusive. Like everything else, this takes creative thinking and detailed planning!

## Balanced ministry

In chapter one, we examined the church's calling to worship, word, witness, warfare and welfare. This means that growing churches have a balanced ministry.

There is something in all people – whatever their age, culture and ethnic background – which needs to worship. But there is also something in all of us which needs warfare. God has given humanity a fighting, competitive spirit.

A balanced ministry touches every area of people's lives and enables them to express every part of their lives. Until recently, many artistic people have not been encouraged to use their skills within the life of the church. This is beginning to change, but we need to allow all talents and all giftings some expression in the church. This will not happen unless we attend to the details which facilitate it.

## Keep focused

We have seen that churches – and especially leaders – need to know where they are going, need to get going, and need to keep going until they get there.

We have to take care that we are not side-tracked, that we keep our direction and focus sharp. This takes constant reviewing and frequent questioning. 'Are we going the right way?' 'Are our programmes working?' 'Are we achieving our goals?' 'Do we need to make changes?' 'What needs strengthening?' 'What needs consolidating?'

Most important of all, we must watch for the creeping paralysis of discouragement. Perseverance is vital. But perseverance is tough! In the short term, there are always many discouragements. But, in the long term, we get there – if we keep going.

In 1 Corinthians 15:58, Paul says: 'Therefore my dear brothers, stand firm, let nothing move you. Always give yourselves fully to the work of the Lord, because you know that your labour in the Lord is not in vain'.

Our work is not in vain because we are going to reap a harvest if we do not faint. Some of us think that we will faint if we do not reap a harvest. But God says, 'Keep at it. Keep focused on the vision. Keep your energy and motivation high. You will win through. Christ really will build his church in your community.'

# QUESTIONS

1. What changes to your church's organisation and structures would facilitate growth? What prevents these changes from being made?

2. What practical and possible changes to your building or meeting-place would make it more accessible, attractive and functional? How can these alterations be implemented?

3. What changes would make your meetings more welcoming, culturally relevant, attractive and challenging to newcomers?

4. In what ways does the leadership of your church need to change so that the membership can be mobilised? How can the mass-mobilisation and training of members become a higher priority?

5. How can your church's preaching and teaching ministry be improved? How can this be discussed positively?

6. What practical changes need to be made so that relationships can be developed and enhanced?

7. What activities have outlived their purpose and need to be ended? How can this be done without unnecessary pain and offence?

# FIVE

# Putting people first

We know that the church is all about God and people. It concerns his relationship with his people, and their relationship with each other.

Those of us who are church leaders, know that we are meant to follow God's example in the way we deal with the people he has given into our care. We know that we should be forgiving, patient, caring, compassionate and gentle.

A few leaders have such a goal-directed ministry that they appear impatient with people. When I listen to some pastors, it seems as if they wish that they could have a church without any people. They seem to think, 'If my church had no people it would be the best church in the world. It would be well run, efficient and effective. But people keep on messing it up for me.'

Humans are extraordinary. They are unpredictable, argumentative and imperfect. But they are also funny and loveable. If we are to lead growing churches, we must love people without any qualifications or pre-conditions. Unbounded love must break out everywhere.

Somehow, we must get people to laugh at themselves and not take themselves too seriously. I think that the capacity to laugh at oneself must be the missing spiritual gift: it really should be in one of the New Testament lists of gifts! But perhaps it is not there because it is a matter of the human will, rather than of supernatural enabling.

When we are gentle with people, they begin to realise that we value them and do not view them as pew-fodder – or chair-fillers. People are not numbers on membership lists. They are not statistics on the way to a full church. People are uniquely valuable. They are packed with divine potential. Each one matters more than any project, any building, any meeting.

We live in a society which continually devalues people. It isolates us socially. It strips us of our humanity. It makes us feel insignificant, unimportant, irrelevant. We all feel much better when we are treated with some respect and importance.

It is wonderful when we are on the telephone to an office or organisation, and feel as though we are being listened to and treated as an individual. We notice when this happens, when – for example – the person at the other end stops reading from their prepared script and starts to listen to us. For a few moments, we know that the person has related to us as a human being. This makes us feel good. This is how we should treat people in the church all the time.

Some church leaders appear to view people as either objects or instruments of their ministry. Others view them as clients or projects. But the people in our churches are brothers and sisters. They are co-equal saints with whom we will spend eternity. Of course, they may hurt and betray us – just as we may damage and disappoint them. But, if we let them, they will bless us and build the church. If we believe that Jesus really did die for them, they must be worth every sacrifice that we make – and many more.

## Always encourage

Growing churches are filled with encouragement. This should not surprise us for encouragement is the essence of the Holy Spirit. In fact, the Greek word for encouragement, *paraklesis*, is a form of the word that Jesus used in John 16:7 when he introduced the Spirit as *parakletos* – the helper, comforter, advocate or encourager.

Encouragement means getting alongside people in the same way that Jesus did – and as the Spirit does. It means gently but persistently urging people on in their lives with God.

Acts 4:36 shows how Joseph of Cyprus was given the 'nickname' Barnabas because he was such an encourager. Acts 11:24 describes Barnabas as 'full of the Holy Spirit', and Acts 9:26-28; 11:19-26; 12:25 – 13:5 show how he went alongside people to encourage them, to train them and to release them in ministry.

If we claim to be filled with the *Parakletos*, it surely follows that we should be characterised by *paraklesis*. If our churches give the *Parakletos* a special place and honour, encouragement should surely be a dominant feature.

This means that, if we care about people with the care of the Spirit, we will affirm them, we will build them, and we will do everything we can to train them and release them in ministry.

As we care for people and encourage them in their gifts, talents and ministries, we should set the highest possible standards in everything we do. If we personally aim for excellence, the people around us will rise to this standard. Obviously we do not want a clinical perfection in our churches which stops people from feeling that they could get involved or that they could make a contribution. But we do want the very best that each person can do.

### Never enslave

Some leaders seem to think that their church would grow if only the people were more committed. They see the problem of stagnation in terms of the people's lack of commitment. They are always saying that their people do not pray enough, do not attend enough, do not give enough, and so on. But growing churches are filled with grace, not condemnation.

Too many church leaders try to hold their people in

some form of bondage. They might preach a message which rightly states that the people can do nothing to *become* saved. But they infer that the people must do many things to *stay* saved. For example, they must belong exclusively to the one congregation. They must attend all the activities. They must pass a commitment course. They must tithe, pray, support prescribed causes, worship in a certain way, believe a vast multitude of tiny details, and so on.

Such leaders think that everything would be all right if everyone did all these things. This is neither a good way to get a response nor is it God's way. We must not forget that our God is a God of grace, and that his church should be characterised by divine grace rather than human legalism.

We must not drive people too hard or too fast, lest they become dissatisfied and resentful. Instead, we must let them go at their own pace. Some leaders have a tendency to try and introduce too much too soon, but lasting change is best accomplished gradually. Few of us can cope with rapid change – we need time to adjust – so we must be patient and work slowly but persistently.

We are all much more impatient than God. We need to recognise how patient he has been with us – how long he has put up with our funny ways and ideas, how long he has tolerated our faults and unhelpful habits. We should not expect people to change any quicker than we have! Instead we should ask God to fill us with his patience and his persistence. Quite often, giving people enough time for the seed of something to grow and develop is the difference between success and failure.

## BUILDING A SUCCESSFUL TEAM

Putting people first is the third key to growth. This involves more than just applying the general principles of leadership that we have examined. We have to put people first in intensely practical ways.

I believe that the most important way we put people

first is by developing teams. We know that growth needs the mobilisation and involvement of the whole church. Personally, I believe this means that there must be team-work at every level in the church.

In a very small church, the whole church will be one team. But as a church grows, a strong team needs to emerge to lead the work. Even so, the entire church can still be organised to function in teams.

At Kensington Temple, I rely very heavily on teamwork and spend a considerable amount of time on team building and training team members. Any church that wants to grow – especially those which want to plant new churches – will focus strongly on building successful teams.

### A team

A team can be defined as a group of people who are organised to work together to achieve a common goal. I think that there are three elements to a team.

Firstly, there must be someone who organises the team: this is the team leader. Teamwork does not make leadership redundant, instead we need committed teams with good leaders.

I think that is rather like a football team. The Holy Spirit is the manager. He decides the vision and strategy, and he tells the team how to play. The leader is the captain. He is in charge on the pitch. He encourages the players as they play, and reminds them of the manager's plan. Each player has a special function – which might vary with every game – but they are all expected to help each other out when necessary.

Secondly, there must be co-operation, because the team is working together. The rationale of a team is that it is better to do something together than apart. In every sport, a well-organised team with tremendous team spirit usually beats a group of highly talented individuals who are not pulling together. This is *synergism* – the truth that we achieve more together than through the sum of our individual efforts.

Thirdly, the team must work together to achieve a common goal. It is vital that the members agree about their vision and strategies. There must be movement and direction – the whole team must know where they are going and what they are trying to do.

Jesus' example in choosing, training and releasing the twelve apostles is the supreme biblical example of team building. He brought them together and worked with them. He taught them how to work in co-operation and gave them something to work towards. He allowed them to make mistakes, but he corrected them when they erred and showed them how to improve.

When we are building a team, it is tempting to choose people whom we like or who are like us. But a team of eleven forwards or eleven goalkeepers will not be very effective. It is better to select a mixture of complimentary abilities and personalities, to set up some interesting dynamics in the team.

It is foolish to choose people who agree with us or who think the same way that we do – this approach demonstrates our insecurity rather than our commitment to teams and church growth.

It is well known that Jesus' twelve apostles were an odd mixture of personalities and backgrounds: there was meticulous Matthew, impetuous Peter, fiery James, cynical Thomas, flawed Judas, and so on.

However, I think that Jesus chose this variety of personalities because they could help each other – even though the mixture must have been frustrating at times.

People who are slow at accepting new ideas balance those who are quick to introduce changes. Those who are creative in their thinking complement those who focus on practical details. We need both types of people in our leadership teams – as long as they recognise and respect each other's special functions! Involving a 'detail' person in creative planning is like asking a goalkeeper to take corners – it's a disaster!

A church leadership team must contain a mixture of ministry strengths. If the leader is a strong Bible teacher, they should ensure that someone with an evangelistic ministry is also on the team. If the leader is a good pastor, they should appoint a gifted administrator to the team, and so on.

This principle applies to all teams in every church. The maintenance team needs a mixture of gifts, personalities and skills, so does the worship team, the children's work team, and every team we develop.

In a small church, the leadership team may include only three people – though I do not think that teams work with less than three. But even the smallest team can contain a balance of personalities, gifts and ministries.

## Team relationships

A successful team is one whose members co-operate fully, and co-operation depends on relationships. Whenever I am involved in a team, one of my highest priorities is developing excellent relationships between all the team members.

I think that there are three factors in good team relationships. Firstly, there needs to be some level of emotional 'bonding' with each other – we need a degree of personal friendship. I find that I work better when I have bonded with people and got to know them as friends as well as colleagues.

I know that some leaders prefer a more 'businesslike' relationship, where the task is more important than the relationship. But I think that people should come before business, meetings, activities, and so on; they should be second only to Jesus.

I find that there is an easier flow of ideas in teams where there is a strong element of friendship between the members. The only weakness in this is that members who like each other too much may not correct each other when necessary. Close relationships should not hinder us from the task. We must remember that no team is an end in itself; it is simply a means of the church growing.

The second factor is that there must be serious commitment between the members. I give strong commitment and I expect it in return – but only so that the job can be done.

From time to time, all team members have personal difficulties and problems. There are periods of time when they are less productive. There are tensions. Commitment makes allowances; it keeps the relationship going – despite the difficulties. There is pain in this, but – if we believe in putting people first – we will look after the people with whom we work.

By 1 Samuel 22, David had been anointed as king but had not been widely recognised. Even so, many discontented and desperate people came to him while he was in the cave of Adullam. Throughout his difficult exile, David worked with these people and moulded them into a team. When he was finally crowned king, in 2 Samuel 2, it was the same people who had stood with him in exile who were standing with him as king.

We can call this sort of committed relationship a 'covenant' type of relationship – and this is what we should encourage between the members of every team in our churches. The catering team need to be just as committed to each other as the leadership team. When we agree together and covenant together within the church, we release the powerful force of unity.

The third factor in a good team relationship is communication. Members should have particular responsibilities, but they must also keep each other informed about the progress of their tasks. Team members should meet formally and informally to keep the lines of communication open in every direction.

I have found that mutual trust and respect develop from good communication. People must know what is going on, for nothing destroys a team like the suspicion of secrecy.

Our organisational structure at Kensington Temple means that some people are in authority and others are more junior. This is necessary from an organisational point of view; but our structure is not the essence of the church itself, rather it is something which facilitates the church.

God's church is about equal relationships – nobody is above or below anyone else, nobody is more or less important – but the church does have to be organised. This organisation is not the church and it must never get in the way of the church, rather it should facilitate it. This is a critical distinction which many leaders miss – they confuse the human organisation with the spiritual reality.

There is no hierarchy in the real church, for there we are essentially one in Jesus. However, there will always be 'bosses' in every human organisation. This practical reality must not interfere with *ekklesia* and *koinonia* in the church.

I recognise that it is hard to combine human organisation with holy church life, but we do it by communicating that every person in the team – whatever their status or position – is worthy of trust and respect and that nobody is superior or more important than anyone else.

We are in it together, and every job is equally important. After all, people do not stay away just because the preaching is poor; they also stop coming if the cleaner leaves the toilets dirty or the steward is rude and unfriendly.

## Pastoral leadership

I believe that the church 'captain' or senior leader should lead from the front. I know that British shepherds have traditionally led their sheep from the rear, but they use dogs to snap at the sheep's heels! Jewish shepherds, however, have always led their sheep from the front, and this is the example commended by Jesus.

I do not believe that team leaders should stand behind the other members of the team, trying to shove and push them on ahead. Biblical leaders stride ahead boldly, setting an example and direction for the others to follow. By their words and actions, they show the way to go – but they do this at a speed which the others can follow. Sheep

## Pierres Vivantes

In December 1990, at a KT reception for Christians in Sport, I was approached by a colleague who needed a French-speaker to help an Angolan family. As I prayed and talked with them, I was surprised to find that they had been Christians for four years yet knew little about the word of God.

After the reception, I couldn't stop thinking about this family. My English was good enough to enable me to follow the services and participate in the church activities. Yet being a Christian is not easy.

God started challenging me to do something among French-speaking believers in London. In April 1991, I approached another lady whom I knew to be French-speaking and together we sought God's will. God spoke to us, and gave us the vision for the work which is still our main thrust today.

Before launching in September 1991 as a church for French-speaking Christians, we met to pray and prepare for six months. We gathered every Saturday afternoon at Kensington Temple, and – during those six months – a core group of 17 people emerged who were committed to the vision and were prepared to pray and to work.

When we launched as a church, we were still meeting at KT, but we moved to the London Embassy Hotel after a year. By then, about 50 people were attending our services and meetings.

At first, we found it difficult to find mature Christians to lead groups. So we concentrated on training the disciples who gathered around us.

We have had a large turnover of members, as many French-speakers are in London only briefly before returning home. Yet we have been able to train them for their return – and have gone on supporting them with books, cassettes and prayer.

We believe God has called us to support mission work in the Francophone world. Our position in London gives us unique opportunities to prepare French-speaking believers who will lead churches in many difficult situations across the world.

Our involvement in the London City Church has been a tremendous strength and blessing. Yet, through their involvement in LCC, some of our members have left us for KT – partly because of the better quality preaching and worship, and partly because their priority is improving their English.

We have had to overcome many obstacles. We have been harassed at the hotel. Some members come from far and pastoral care is hard. 16 countries are represented, so cultural misunderstanding is easy. Yet God has blessed us with growth. By 1996, about 200 people were meeting each Sunday in two congregations, north and south of the Thames.

*Pastor Kemi Ajayi*

cannot follow a shepherd who has disappeared over the horizon!

This means that we must know where we are going! Vision and leadership cannot be separated. However, it does not mean either that we must know all the answers or that we must provide all the answers. Rather, the team leader merely accepts the responsibility of saying, 'Yes, that's the answer. You are right. That is the way we should go.'

It takes mature and secure leadership to accept and apply the truth that the answer to a church's dilemma may come from the tiniest member of the Sunday School. Believe me; words often come from God through the most unlikely members of the congregation. But it is the responsibility of leadership to recognise when this is from God and to lead the people into it.

If leaders are to lead from the front, it is clear that they must have a forward looking attitude. Team leaders need to live in the future. I sometimes put the wrong year down when I write the date on a letter or cheque. I am not absent-minded, I am just always thinking several years in the future.

Team members will be pre-occupied with the detail of their responsibilities. The leader needs to inspire them with the big vision, with the purpose behind their efforts. He or she needs to encourage them to keep their eyes fixed on the goal. Hebrews 12:2 reports that Jesus endured the cross because of the joy which was to come. It was his vision of his goal which enabled him to keep going.

As a team leader, I feel a keen responsibility of helping the members develop their full potential. I believe that God holds me responsible for their spiritual development and for the realisation of their ministry potential.

This is not always easy, as the needs of the organisation require that some members have to be patient. It might be obvious that a member's strength lies in one area, yet they have to work in a different area because the team as a whole is weak there. If we reserve the right to deploy people, they must be deployed in a way which best meets the needs of the whole organisation. However, this must be balanced against the need to match people's work with their giftings.

Of course, some young leaders will always find it difficult when they are held back from their personal preferences. But we must constantly encourage them to see and to serve a bigger vision than their own career plan.

When I came out of Bible College, I worked in a drug rehabilitation centre. Although I had a burning desire to preach and teach, my principal responsibilities were practical – and many of them were not at all pleasant! On reflection, I can see that it was a very important phase of character building. The fact that I had to hold back from what I considered my real ministry meant that I learned the vital lesson of sacrifice.

I suspect that one of the most important lessons we have to learn is the need to sacrifice our love for our ministry. We have to put it to death – remembering that there is a resurrection ahead. As we develop in God, so he entrusts us with greater responsibilities in the Spirit.

Team leaders have to behave like Jesus with the twelve. He watched them making mistakes and listened to them saying ridiculous things without crushing their enthusiasm and commitment. It was as if he thought, 'There's Peter. One day he's going to be a significant apostle in the church, but right now he's playing the fool. It's only a stage that is passing; I'm not going to smash him.'

Jesus often told the disciples that he had a lot to teach them, but that he could not tell them everything at that moment. He informed Peter that he would be trusted with martyrdom, but he only passed on this news near the end of his ministry. Peter could not have handled the information at the start. Team leaders need a similar sensitivity to the Holy Spirit.

As leaders patiently care for the people in their team, God shows us things which it is not appropriate to share. However, these flashes of insight should play a part in the way that we allocate responsibilities and give opportunities for service.

Although I often fall short of the standards I set for myself as a team leader, I always consider it a fantastic privilege to develop the potential of team members. I try to offer each member of the team my encouragement and trust. I endeavour not to stifle their initiatives. I give them responsibility, build in accountability, and try to be available and approachable. Most important of all, I do my best to maintain communication by listening to them and keeping them informed.

Whatever a team's inherent weaknesses and limitations may be, I find that every team flourishes and functions best when communication flows freely between the leader and all the team members.

### Team membership

Every team depends on its members. No one member is less important than any other member, so it is vital that each individual learns to function as part of a team.

For myself, I prize loyalty and faithfulness in teamwork above all else. If we stand together, and are loyal both to each other and to the vision, we will attain the goal that God has given us.

Team members are in a special position to stop bad communication from spreading through the team – and from the team to the wider church. A negative spirit can creep in whenever there is criticism, grumbling or any negative speaking. The member who refuses to listen to a negative communication kills it stone dead.

Moses organised the children of Israel into teams, but his system did not work. It was well organised, but he still became exhausted. Numbers 11:11-25 reports how God then said that he would take of the Spirit which was upon Moses and put the same on the elders. When that happened, the members of Moses' team in essence also caught his spirit. From then on, the Bible does not report Moses complaining of an inability to lead such a vast number of people.

Members of a team must try to 'catch the spirit' of the leader. In too many church groups, an inspired leader is surrounded by a team who seem to be implementing the leader's vision without his spirit. They appear to perform their responsibilities harshly – without the same gentleness, flexibility and humility as the leader.

People often ask me how I manage to lead a church which is so large and diverse. It is simply because I have such a good group of men and women on the leadership team – and I spend a great deal of time inputting into their lives. I pray with them at every opportunity. They know that it is more important for them to catch my spirit than just to repeat my words.

When the members share the leader's attitude and spirit, the church can become more than an organisation and more than a mechanical structure. It can become a living, dynamic, growing organism which is controlled by Christ and characterised by the Holy, humble, self-effacing Spirit.

### Leadership in a small church

Leaders in small churches are often inexperienced, and they have to lead the church with few other leaders and few workers. It is hard for these leaders to delegate as they have so few people to delegate to!

Some people will not join a new church because they are looking for something more established. They want to be part of a church which has a functioning crèche, a flourishing children's work, and a fabulous worship team. They will contribute to something which is already in place, but few are willing to help develop something new.

It is no good when leaders in small churches bemoan what they do not have. All this achieves is a negative mindset which prevents us from doing the best we can with what we have. We have to begin with what we have and depend on the Lord to lead us forward.

We need to pray for workers – as Jesus instructed. God is faithful, he will provide labourers for the harvest. As with so much, this will require persistence. We will need to go on praying to show God how serious we are about his church.

Leaders of small churches need to learn to be self-starters. This means having the ability to think of an idea and get it off the ground. It takes a lot of effort to build something out of nothing.

But we also need to learn to be self-finishers. If starting something new is hard, completing it is even harder. Jesus is both the author and the finisher of our faith and he will help us see things through.

Getting new ideas off the ground can become self-defeating unless some of these ideas are brought to a conclusion. It is better to start with a few things and to see them through, than to start new ideas and programmes every month.

Leaders of small churches need to watch that they do not become overloaded. There is a temptation to go for too much too soon, but this just wears everybody out. People in the church can become tired, and this is often misinterpreted by leaders as unwillingness – who then berate them for their lack of commitment and coldness. It is better to set small achievable tasks and encourage them through to completion, before going on to the next thing.

There is a key to growth in every situation. If we are sensitive to the Spirit, he will show us – in his time! The vision may be very big – even larger then life – but the implementation is slow and painful.

Leaders need to have a definite year-by-year plan. This must be going somewhere, taking people on stage by stage. There must be clear 'by when' dates so that the vision can be worked out in a time-sensitive manner.

Leaders in small churches must take steps to develop and encourage a basic team of key people who provide practical and spiritual support. At the very least, we need someone who is capable of handling the practical details and someone who can help with the worship, preaching and mission. This three-fold cord of leader plus practical plus spiritual support is a basic leadership team for any church.

However, we must let leaders emerge naturally. A hasty appointment usually leads to quick disappointment. We need to identify possible leaders or workers and begin to train and encourage them. Usually, this means nothing more than spending time with them, doing the basic tasks of the church with them and gradually passing on skills – almost without them realising what we are doing.

At some stage, it will be good to develop a modest but effective leadership training programme. It will probably be wise to get help from outside the church. For example, in the London City Church Network we have the benefit of outside teachers as well as a fully fledged training programme.

## BUILDING COMMITMENT IN THE CHURCH

We have seen that church growth requires leaders to establish the church's vision, to attend to the small details and to put people first. These three keys for opening the church doors must be held together. However, in our enthusiasm for visionary teams, flexible buildings and inspired meetings, we must not forget that church growth is not a theory or a method – it is people coming to Jesus.

Church growth depends on church members being mobilised for mission and released in ministry. It depends on unsaved people being attracted to the wider life of the church. And it depends on new converts being integrated into the church.

I often ask church leaders to imagine how large their churches would be if everyone who had ever passed through the doors had kept on attending. We would all have enormous churches! But this is not reality.

Recent research has shown that only one in five of visitors returns a second time. However, three out of five visitors return when they are contacted within forty-eight hours of their first visit. This has convinced us that it is critical to have some kind of personal contact within two days of a person's initial visit.

This should be an unobtrusive brief greeting. I encourage our home visitors to say something like this: 'I just wanted to let you know how much we appreciated you being with us on Sunday. Thank you for filling out the form or for speaking to so-and-so. We are here for you, and are always available to help. Here is a small booklet for you. It would be really good to see you again some time soon.'

This sort of casual unpressurised contact helps people to feel at ease in the fellowship – as long as the member making the contact recognises and acknowledges the visitor when they return!

In Kensington Temple, working as we do with many overseas groups, we have to be sensitive to those who want to remain largely anonymous. Some visitors are reluctant to give their names and addresses because of their refugee status or other difficulties. Nevertheless, a warm welcome and sensitive follow-up quickly lead to trust being built and a relationship being established.

I know that this is demanding. But if we are serious about growth, and serious about salvation, we will make the necessary sacrifices to put people first in small practical ways like this.

## Welcome

It is very important that we ask ourselves whether we would find it easy to become part of our church if we were newcomers.

As we have seen, every church tends to become a self-perpetuating primary group with its own history and ethos. It grows to a certain size, becomes comfortable, and then ceases to grow. It gets stuck at a certain point, at which only a burglar can break in!

Although the church may say that it exists for newcomers, and the leader offers a verbal 'welcome' at each service, the unconscious reality is different. Members are more interested in talking to their church friends than in relating to visitors. Inadvertently, the newcomer feels frozen out as an intruder.

This has nothing to do with size! In fact, people often

feel more like an intruder in a small church than in a large one. I have even known it to happen in fellowships which are only a few weeks old.

As leaders, we must be aware of this problem and devise ways of dealing with it. It really is not easy for newcomers to get accustomed to a church. They usually start finding their identity with just two or three other people before this is extended to the wider group. We have to be practical to make this process as smooth as possible.

We may need ushers outside the building to help people find the hall or the room. We may need a welcome team to introduce people to a linking member. I know one church which has a hospitality team ready at each service, and all visitors are offered lunch in a family home. Members must, however, be sensitive to the shyness and uncertainties of newcomers and not act like lions pouncing on their prey!

Every now and then, all leaders should deliberately visit a church where they are not known – somewhere outside their normal environment. It is good to see what it feels like to be an outsider, to know nobody when everyone else seems to know everybody, to appreciate how newcomers probably feel in our church!

I think that it is best to have many different ways for visitors to become involved. We need to think about the type of people who are coming and to list all the different routes through which they can be integrated. If there are not enough existing ways, we need to find some more. Hospitality is often the quickest and best way to integration.

Some people may go on attending one service a week for many years and never get involved because they never feel truly 'at home'. They – and newcomers – will be integrated into church life only through a multiplicity of small groups and activities like meals, special projects and outings.

## Portuguese-Speaking Churches

Over several years, I recognised the need for a Portuguese-speaking church in London. There were more than 70,000 Portuguese, Brazilians and Angolans in London. Many of them had fled from civil wars in Africa, and they did not have a place of worship in their own language.

God gave my wife and I a considerable burden for our own people, and we took this as confirmation that we should facilitate a church.

Our vision was to establish a strong Spirit-filled Portuguese speaking church in the heart of London. Our strategy was to establish a base where Portuguese-speaking people could receive help with immigration, accommodation, academic studies, legal matters, personal counselling – and where they could experience God's love and power.

We started small. There were only 8 adults at our first service. But we knew that it would be difficult and we were not discouraged.

We began witnessing in the places where Portuguese speakers meet. Through advertisements and news reports, we spread the message in Brazilian Newspapers that *'There is a Portuguese Speaking Church who Cares'*.

Gradually, the Portuguese-speaking community recognised our presence. The Brazilian consulate and the Brazilian Embassy took notice. They began to refer people to us who had 'spiritual needs'. This was one factor in our rapid church growth.

The men and women who were referred to us were becoming saved – and then they were bringing others to Christ. So much so, that – by the end of the first year – over 100 adults were part of the church.

My wife and I consider the help of the London City Church Network to have been very important in establishing the work. The leaders have guided and advised us. They contributed to some specific financial needs. And their backing meant that we could obtain visas more easily – especially for Pastors from overseas.

We share the LCC Network's vision for church planting, and are sure that this is the best way to reach the Portuguese community in London.

Since the initial church in Central London, we have managed to plant 9 more churches in various parts of London where there are concentrations of Portuguese speakers.

Right from the start, we have had a vision to reach Portuguese-speakers throughout Europe. We have begun to fulfil this by planting a church in Brussels.

In addition to this, we have also developed a Portuguese-speaking Bible School where believers can be grounded in the faith and trained for ministry.

*Pastor Enoque Pereira*

## Integration

As leaders, we must be diligent and committed to finding
ways of integrating people into the life of the church. Yet
our job does not end there. When they are integrated, we
need to mobilise them and thrust them out into the work
of God.

People start attending church services for a variety of
reasons. But they will be integrated into the church only
when they have a sense of belonging. This develops
through relationships which are forged, fostered and nurtured by the Holy Spirit.

We must help people become a real part of the church.
But we will not achieve this by preaching against their
lack of commitment – demands for commitment usually
result in an outward adherence which is just legalistic
bondage.

Instead, people will be integrated into the life of the
church through their involvement in relevant and meaningful relationships. Remember, *koinonia* is at the heart of
the church; so we need to be diligent in creating a variety
of activities and groups which offer people the opportunity of belonging and participating.

Ideally, there should be enough groups in the church
for everyone to feel comfortable in one. When there is
something suitable for everyone, people are more likely
to stay and become part of the fellowship.

This often means forming groups along professional
lines such as teachers and nurses, or establishing groups
on age or ethnic lines. Please remember that people are
most likely to be won for Christ along lines of common
interest and kinship.

No church is too small to divide into appropriate
groups. Personally, I think that it is an excellent goal for
every church to see everyone involved in one small
group. As people are grafted into the life of the fellowship
so they begin to produce fruit – when the life of the
church is flowing through them.

There has been a tremendous change in society, with

much greater mobility. For example, many people now buy their household goods at a large supermarket, their meat at a local butcher, and their vegetables at a street market. In the same way, some Christians think nothing about attending one church in the morning, another in the evening, and a third mid-week.

At one level, this can help people appreciate the essential 'unity in diversity' of the church. But I believe that we need to be integrated into one community church. This integration should not prevent us from being involved in the wider 'local' church; rather it is the foundation of that involvement.

People need to be encouraged to find their God-appointed place in the body of Christ – and I am convinced this means a certain fellowship, in a particular place, under a specific ministry.

Once a believer is called to a particular fellowship, it is the leaders responsibility to cultivate and nurture their fellowship, and to work with them for the good of the church. Once God has placed us in a community church, we have no reason or liberty to leave until God clearly moves us on. However, we must be careful that it really is God, and not our own impatience or unwillingness to persevere through a particular difficulty.

I find that people become fully integrated when they are inspired by the church's vision. Church leaders should constantly hold up the church's vision to the people: 'This is what God has called us to do, and this is how we are doing it'.

At Kensington Temple, I frequently say, 'Our vision is to win London and the world for Jesus. In order to do this, our vision is to become a fully functioning city church by the end of the decade. We will achieve this by establishing a network of 2,000 groups and churches.'

Many people who hear this feel something rising within them saying, 'Yes!' These are the people I want. They will run with me. They will sweat with me. They will weep with me. Together, we will hear the Spirit speaking to us – guiding, empowering and encouraging us on towards the vision.

Equally, there are people who feel nothing. They say to themselves, 'This really isn't for me!' Instead God is calling them to a different place in the body, and we need to encourage them to find that place of service.

## *Nurture*

All leaders need to ask themselves whether their church meets their people's needs. Does it really have something for all the people who attend, and for those we are seeking to attract. In too many churches, the needs of a past generation are being met rather than the real needs of the members today.

Every person who attends the church – including the team leader – needs to be built up. Through the media, we are all bombarded every day with godless opinions and ideas.

In this world of trouble, we all need to know that there is a God who is real, who cares and is dependable. In this age of shifting materialistic and immoral values, we need to know that there is a sold rock, a strong foundation for life, in Jesus Christ.

We need to develop creative and effective ways of teaching the truths and principles of Christianity. Most congregations contain an incredible range of intellects, so we need preaching and teaching which is simple without being simplistic, and which is practical without being patronising.

Everybody who attends church also needs fellowship – genuine biblical *koinonia*. Modern life, especially in our cities, is increasingly alien. Neighbours do not relate. Families are separated by divorce and distance. The church must provide the fellowship which is absent in the world.

The church is a family, yet there is precious little contact between people in some church services. People can sit near each other for an hour or more a week for several years, and still not know each other's names. I cannot stress enough that we must work hard at creating fellowship – genuine people contact – in our churches.

People are crying out for friendship, for love, for contact, for affirmation and communication. They need this as much as they need sermons. As leaders, we must creatively structure our church life so that we meet this desperate need.

Every believer in every church has a basic need to serve Jesus. If we want our church to grow, if we want to put people first, we will meet this need.

The first thing we can do is draw up a list of all the jobs which need doing in our church. This can be everything from making coffee, working the projector and collecting the books, to leading a small group or contacting the bereaved.

Next we can ask ourselves who in the church could be linked with these activities. Then we plan training.

We used to have an annual Kensington Temple training day when we invited everyone who wanted to be involved in the work of the church. We gave a seminar on stewardship, listed the jobs which needed people, and then gave the training requirements. Hundreds came each year, and we filled all the church's job vacancies for the next twelve months in one weekend. Now that we are larger, this process takes place throughout the whole year.

This sort of approach gets people involved, frees the leaders for prayer and preparation, and facilitates growth.

Please never forget that the first job of leaders is to help people discover their ministry, to equip people for ministry, to release people in ministry and to service them in ministry.

People are eternally grateful to leaders who act like this. I am so indebted to the man who let me serve in a home for drug rehabilitation. He started me off in ministry, and I will always be thankful to him for trusting me. I am sure that he would have found it much easier and quicker to do the job himself. But he knew that his calling as a Christian leader was to equip the saints for the work of ministry – not to do it for them.

## *Three keys to growth*

By now, we should have seen that there are three keys to
church growth. And we should have grasped that those
who long to breakthrough into significant growth do not
choose between the keys. They grasp all three and hold
them in balance.

We have seen that we must receive, develop and constantly explain God's vision for the church. We understand
that we must attend to the small details of church life
which make a big difference to growth. And we appreciate that people have to be central to all we do and think.
From now on, caring for people's real needs will be our
highest priority.

I hope we are convinced that we minister with the confidence of Jesus' victory. I trust we are certain that Jesus
has promised to build his church in our community. And
I pray that we are committed to translating his victory and
his promise into church growth – through conversions –
in each of our localities.

Please join me in declaring that this will be our main
pre-occupation; and that we will do our utmost to ensure
that it is the chief purpose in life of every member of all
our churches.

# QUESTIONS

1. What needs to change for it to become more obvious that people come first in your church?

2. What gifts, strengths and weaknesses exist in each leadership group in your church? How can the teams become better balanced?

3. In what way are the different leadership groups not united in heart, vision and purpose? How can this be rectified?

4. What provision is made for the training and development of the leaders? How can the leaders continue their personal and spiritual growth?

5. What practical steps can be taken to make visitors feel more welcome and to integrate newcomers?

6. What pastoral care structures need to be put in place so that every person is pastored and finds a niche within the fellowship?

7. How does your church need to change so that it cares more for newcomers than the comfort and convenience of its members?

## SIX

# Creative evangelism

We noted in chapter four that creative planning is one of a Christian leader's primary responsibilities. This is particularly true of evangelism.

In the last few years, I have noticed that some churches are wasting time, money and energy in forms of evangelism which rarely or never reach people. They succeed only in discouraging believers by their lack of results.

We cannot be committed to church growth without being involved in evangelism. Yet many churches lack flair and creativity when they think about sharing their faith. We must use our God-given creativity. We must seek God's will. And we must be honest about the effectiveness of whatever means we choose to use.

Each individual church has its own unique character, and is capable of reaching a particular group of people. This means that an evangelistic tool which works well at one time in one church may fail in another. There is no 'right' method for every church – the Spirit honours a vast number of approaches.

Over the years at Kensington Temple, we seem to have tried just about everything! Obviously, with such a large congregation we can arrange regular 'set piece' events which have a high standard of performance. We use the dramatic and musical skills of a few gifted members to arrange evangelistic plays and concerts which attract large audiences. Several thousand people have come to Christ through these 'gospel shows'. In fact, the well-known drama, 'Heaven's Gates, Hell's Flames' has been the most effective evangelistic tool we have known.

As well as occasional shows, we hold regular evangelistic services, healing and deliverance meetings, and enquirers and seekers services. These follow a more traditional format with singing, prayers, testimonies, sermon and ministry.

However, most people who are converted at our special evangelistic events have already been warmed to the gospel through other less visible evangelistic activities. We do not prepare a show, print some publicity, put up a few posters, and then wait for the sinners to turn up.

Instead our younger members are encouraged to be involved with activities like gardening, shopping, car washing, baby sitting, and so on. Older members are urged to participate in community affairs like neighbourhood watch, jumble sales, craft fairs, parents' groups, and tenants' meetings.

It is precisely the people who are contacted through these low profile activities who are personally invited to our special events. It is they who turn to Christ. The special meetings may catch the eye, but they merely 'reap' what has slowly grown from our patient unseen 'sowing'.

Any church can 'sow' in a wide variety of ways. We can organise crèches for shoppers, talks and debates on topical issues, and English language training for overseas students.

We can help at old people's homes and rehabilitation centres. We can arrange special lunches at Christmas, Passover, Chinese New Year, and so on. We can run children's clubs, parents' advice evenings and day centres for the unemployed.

We can distribute Christian books, videos, cassettes and newspapers. We can advertise in local newspapers, carry out questionnaires and surveys, organise Christian Unions in local colleges, prisons, hospitals, factories and offices, and run coffee mornings for people in their homes.

I recognise that, usually, only large congregations can put on special evangelistic events which cater for thousands. But these will be only 'Christian entertainment' unless the people in those congregations have unsaved contacts whom they befriend and invite.

Leaders often ask me why so many people are saved at our evangelistic meetings. The answer is simple. It is because our members bring so many unsaved people along whom they have contacted, prayed for, cared for, befriended, witnessed sensitively to, and so on.

Any small church can be involved in a whole host of evangelistic activities. They can do most of what we have done, if on a smaller scale. But their activities will be fruitful only if their church members are eager and equipped to reach out with the gospel.

The majority of congregations in the London City Church Network have about fifty members. They face exactly the same difficulties as every small church, but they are growing. Why? Because most of the people in every congregation are being mobilised and trained in evangelism.

No army should ever go into battle without adequate training. No serious athlete would dream of arriving at a competition without adequate training. In the same way, no Christian should be sent into the world with the gospel without proper training.

Thorough and effective training in evangelism must be the most obvious requirement for any church which wants to grow. Growth does not come out of thin air – people have to be contacted and converted.

Congregations in the London City Church Network have found three evangelistic programmes particularly helpful. Churches of any size could use these or adapt them to suit their special needs.

## *Evangelism Explosion*

Evangelism Explosion (EE) is a training programme which is designed for local church evangelism. Many churches I know have described it as life-transforming. Its founder saw his church in the United States grow from just nineteen people to over 8,000. British churches which use EE have not experienced the same degree of growth, but they have found it helpful. Today, the programme is being used in churches of every denomination in over 150 countries.

There are three key reasons why I think that EE is an ideal tool for training in preparation for growth. It is church based. It equips every believer. It provides essential practical experience – by the end of the EE training programme, people are equipped to present the gospel, to deal with objections, to lead a person to Christ, to disciple new believers – and to help others do the same.

EE is not just another theoretical Bible study course in evangelism. Using an apprenticeship method, people not only receive good teaching through EE, they also reach out and share their faith.

If a church wants to use EE, one if its leaders must first attend a Leaders' Training Course where they can be trained to teach the programme. This is a short intensive course which is held at regular intervals in most countries.

Once a church leader has qualified to teach EE, a small group of members meets together one evening a week for twelve weeks. They study, learn some scriptural gospel presentations, and go out with the leader to witness. When the course is finished, the people who have been trained become trainers and start to teach others.

EE makes great use of the Bible and testimonies. I find that church members who have been trained through EE are much better equipped to reach people and to chat with them sensitively about the gospel.

EE encourages believers to use two basic questions which seem to get to the heart of the matter. Firstly, 'Have you come to a place in your life where you can say for certain that, if you die tonight, you will go to heaven?' And secondly, 'Supposing you were to die tonight and stood before God, what would you say if God asked you why he should let you into his heaven?'

Obviously we have to rephrase the questions so that we are comfortable with them, and they are relevant to the person we are talking to. And, of course, we have to use them sensitively and in a proper context. Even so, we have found that EE training gives our members confidence and resources which – when they are used under the Spirit's control and direction – have helped many to turn to Christ.

### Alpha

The Alpha course is one of the most recent and successful evangelistic programmes. It was developed by Holy Trinity, Brompton, the well-known Anglican church in London, and has brought many people to Christ. Smaller churches, in particular, have found it especially helpful.

Alpha is a practical introduction to the Christian faith. It occupies ten weeks and is targeted primarily at seekers, enquirers and people on the fringe of the church. It is an excellent 'follow-up' for people who have been contacted through EE or through the general work of the church.

Our experience of Alpha at Kensington Temple suggests that it helps outsiders to feel at ease and to be able to participate. The welcome, food, seating, small groups and talks all help people find faith. Everyone is allowed to ask whatever they like. No question is seen as too trivial, illogical or threatening. We try to ensure that every answer is given courteously and thoughtfully.

Each Alpha session begins with a snack served on laps in small groups. Then there is the talk to the whole group, which is followed by coffee and questions in small groups.

The ten session course is a basic biblical introduction to Christianity which is Christ centred. It ends with a supper party or, in our case, a breakfast party – to which people are encouraged to bring their friends. We have found that Alpha helps people to make quality relationships and to be integrated into the church.

## Good News Down The Street

Although we make good use of EE and Alpha, many other evangelistic programmes are also followed in the London City Church Network.

One of our congregations has used and adapted a simple programme called 'Good News Down The Street'. This lasts for only six weeks, is based in homes or offices, and each individual session never takes more than an hour.

Church members invite contacts to learn about their faith. Three Christians are involved – one as leader and two training to lead. The members who are learning to lead are expected to lead the next course!

There is no talk. Instead, in each session, the visitors are asked a series of simple questions. For example, they are asked whether they think Jesus is a good man, a prophet, a Son of God or an astronaut. Whatever they reply, the leader responds with something like, 'That's interesting, now let us see what the Bible says'.

There is never any argument. The leader simply asks questions, listens to the answers, and then leads a very short Bible study which is based on the people's answers. We are always out of the home in under an hour. This means that no visit is intimidating, and the course can be fitted into a lunch hour or around shift work.

All of the structured programmes I have outlined have four outstanding advantages. They train and release members in evangelism. They introduce people to Jesus. They bring discipline and order into a church's evangelism programme. And they integrate outsiders into church life.

There are a vast number of other approaches to evangelism. However, I think that they can all be helpfully classified in five main groups. It is my belief that any church which seriously wants to grow should always have some involvement in each of the five areas. We should not

## Wembley Christian Fellowship

In January 1991, we began praying about our next step in ministry. As we waited on God for direction we spent much time praying in tongues and in spiritual warfare. We later realised that God was birthing a church in us through our praying.

Soke Mun is also a dentist, and her surgery is strategically placed in the middle of the area we now pastor. This has been the key into the community for the church. In the Spring of 91, several people were converted in the surgery – including a heroin addict – and we realised the need for a fellowship which would care for these converts.

We continued to pray until God told us, 'Go for it! This is the time' He impressed Isaiah 61:1-3 on us, and this has been our mandate.

The church began in January 1992 at The Lord's Bar – a pub in Wembley Park. Soke Mun and I began with a group of 10 people and started praying for and evangelising the area.

People quickly joined us, but some had their own agendas. One by one, after much prayer, people started leaving. After a period, the church began to consolidate and to grow from strength to strength.

We organised our first evangelistic mission in the summer of 1993 – and the church halved in size! It took us three months to recover from learning how not to run a mission. Happily, our next mission in 1994 proved to be extremely beneficial.

We have had some struggles with our premises. First, the landlord tried to throw us out; then he quadrupled the rent. But God over-ruled and has helped us to stay there. A psychic fair, which hired the room next door, has had to leave instead!

Early on, Soke Mun and I were given a prophecy that we would be like spiritual mid-wives – and that has proved accurate. Many have come to Christ. We have found *Evangelism Explosion* to be a vital harvesting tool, and the whole fellowship is learning to present the gospel effectively.

Early on, 80% of the church had been Christians for less than 2 years. This created its own problems, as there were few mature Christians, and Soke Mun and I had to learn fast to be effective pastors.

However, we have had much support from the LCC Network. We receive a lot of practical advice, support and teaching. As we partner with the network's vision and submit to the leadership of KT, we find that we share the network's anointing for growth and church planting.

Our vision is to impact the community by meeting the needs of the people through crèches, drug centres and other relevant ministries. We now have a vision to plant four more churches in the area – and the first has been launched. After almost five years work, 40 adults worship at *The Lord's Bar* – and we look for more growth in the future.

*Pastors Vanessa Richardson & Soke Mun Ho*

pick and choose between them – creative evangelism uses a rich and complementary mixture of approaches.

## *Friendship evangelism*

All the most successful forms of evangelism are based on friendship – on us reaching out to people whom we already know. Many Christians – especially leaders – think that they are committed to evangelism, but they see little lasting fruit because they have few unsaved friends.

Some church leaders make this problem worse by arranging church meetings on almost every night of the week and urging their members to attend. It is little wonder that some believers lose contact with their unsaved friends and become unsuccessful soul-winners!

At Kensington Temple, we encourage all our members along the lines of 'each one reach one'. It is easy for believers to be paralysed by the needs of all the different people they know. So we ask our people prayerfully to focus on only two or three of their unsaved relatives and friends – and to commit themselves to reaching one of them with the gospel during the year.

If all our members followed this, our church would double in size every year – in fact, we would convert the whole of London in under ten years!

Our people ask the Spirit to show them whom they should particularly pray for during the year. Members then support each other in prayer – especially in small groups – and together we look for ways of reaching the folk we have identified. When this simple idea is well organised, it significantly encourages and builds the church.

We find that the home is the best place for friendship evangelism. A bite to eat and a sociable conversation are the ideal environment for people to relax and talk about the gospel.

For example, our Japanese church has found that Japanese students in London are starved of Japanese food. They rarely turn down an invitation to a Japanese buffet style meal. Our members show a genuine interest in the lives of the students, contacts are made, friendships begun, and the gospel is soon shared.

We are not looking for instant commitments at these meals. Rather we are seeking to build genuine friendships and to 'sow' gospel thoughts which the Spirit can use in the future. However, friendships made at the meal table can be 'reaped' later. These are the folk who are most likely to respond to an invitation to a special evangelistic meeting – and to respond to Christ's claims at that meeting.

### Street work

There are various kinds of street evangelism. In the past, many churches held open-air meetings and knocked on doors to tell people about the gospel. We still have teams witnessing at Portobello Market and through the night in Leicester Square.

Over the years, these teams have seen people converted nearly every week. Not all of the converts have joined us, as many of them have been tourists or visitors who have had to be linked with churches in their own areas.

The recent increase in 'street-people', however, has meant that a much larger proportion of the converts has started to link with us, and this ministry is currently being extremely fruitful.

In many parts of Britain, open-air preaching is not a useful method today. This has led some of our groups to distribute free Christian newspapers or invitations to special events. Others use questionnaires to prompt conversations. A few have regular market stalls where they sell books, videos, Third World products and 'Fair Trade' goods.

One of our churches uses the electoral roll to write to all the homes in a street before visiting them. In the letter, they introduce themselves, say that they are going to call, and explain that they want to pray for the homes in that road. This initiative has had a very positive response in the community.

I believe that some form of street work is particularly important for new churches – especially those which do not have the full-time use of a recognised building. It gives them a chance to learn local needs and make useful contacts. Given persistence, sensitivity and common sense, this sort of evangelism helps to build trust in a community.

## Social events

Church barbecues, garden fetes, picnics and parties are gentle ways of inviting friends into a Christian atmosphere. We find that these sorts of events help to break down misconceptions about Christianity and to provide a platform for a sensitive introduction to the faith.

At Kensington Temple, we have even started a sports club. This is a place where Christians and non-Christians can swim, play squash and exercise together. Two-thirds of the attenders are not yet saved – but they are receptive to invitations to special evangelistic events.

In the past, some evangelical churches would not have considered running a sports club to be part of their evangelism. We think, however, that we must be involved in as many different activities as possible which are relevant to the people groups we are targeting. Our focus on singles means that it would be ridiculous if we neglected those who can be befriended and reached through sporting activities.

## Celebration events

Our churches have found that times of celebration are a wonderful opportunity for friends and neighbours to hear the gospel.

Christmas, Easter, Mothers' Day, Harvest Festival, baptisms, birthdays – even funerals – bring people together and are a good setting for a brief testimony. However, we should never browbeat a captive audience – one insensitive sermon can put back the cause of the gospel for years.

## Caring activities

Perhaps the most specific way we can show Jesus' love is by caring enterprises and initiatives. Many of us grew up believing that evangelism had nothing to do with social concern; whereas we now realise that these are complementary ways of revealing God's love.

Several churches in the London City Church Network reach out to the homeless. Others support groups like drug addicts and difficult young people. Many provide facilities for Mothers and Toddlers. We have a special team which reaches out to Old People's Homes. Several of our ethnic-based churches are serving immigrant groups in a variety of practical and caring ways.

Of course, none of these approaches to evangelism will be effective without prayer. Sensible, specific, Spirit-directed prayer must undergird all our evangelism. The enemy will tempt us to think either that we are too busy evangelising to pray or that we are so fervent in our praying we need not evangelise. But our churches will never grow unless we both pray *and* share our faith.

In our churches, we must watch out that we never become satisfied with our size. When a church starts to grow, it usually attracts members from other churches. This looks like growth, but – as we have seen – is not. When our buildings become comfortably full, we are tempted to ease off the evangelistic effort. But that is the exact time when we need to examine our structures and strategies so that we can move on from growth into multiplication.

At least 10,000 people are part of the London City Church Network, and about half of these are attached to the central church at Kensington Temple. This may seem large by British standards, yet there are eight million people in London. For all our size and growth, we are merely a tiny drop in the capital bucket!

In fact, we have roughly the same size, relevance and impact on our city as a congregation of two adults and one child in a village with 2,000 people. We really do have absolutely nothing to feel complacent about. We are hardly even scratching the surface.

## Power to grow

Maybe it is because we are a minority in society, but many believers are intimidated by the possible negative reactions of outsiders. We draw back, with a mixture of shame and fear, and try to show our message by goodness alone.

I am convinced that we need to overcome this fear by receiving the power of the Holy Spirit and the boldness which comes only from him.

The early church were a far smaller minority – and faced more violent opposition than many of us in the West today. Yet Acts 3:20 shows us that, when the first disciples were filled with the Spirit's power, they could not help but speak about what they had seen and heard. And, in Romans 1:16, Paul reminds us that he was not ashamed of the gospel because it was the power of God for salvation.

Our shame strips us of power, and insults the One who bought us with his blood. But divine faith and holy boldness destroy all human shame.

As we consider the present situation of our church, we must not give in to unbelief. If God has called us to a task, and we press on in faith, God's will shall be done. We can walk into the harvest field full of his holy self-confidence.

In his power and authority, together we can act as Jesus' hands, legs and mouth. We can reveal the heart and compassion of God. We can work God's works and attract people by our lives to listen to his words.

Like the church of Acts, we need eagerly to desire spiritual gifts and believe that God will use us 'supernaturally'. Mark 16:15-20 show us that Jesus worked with the first disciples when they went out to preach the good news – and that he confirmed their words with holy signs.

Jesus is always true to his word and his nature. He cannot but do the same when we go out too. I know that the work of evangelism is not easy in our sophisticated unbelieving society. But – with prayer, faith, boldness and holy creativity – we can see the entire church trained and released. We can pass on the good news. We can see God's blessing on our outreach to the lost. We can see his church grow.

The time for reading and reflection is over. It is time for visionary action. The day of stagnation and consolidation is over. It is time for significant growth.

Let us consider how we can spur each other on. Let us throw off everything that hinders us. Let us fix our eyes on Jesus so that we do not grow weary and lose heart. God has promised that – at the proper time – we will reap a harvest if we do not give up. Now, I believe, is that proper time for his church in our land. Now is the time for growth and for harvest.

# QUESTIONS

1. What evangelistic activities has your church tried in the last two years? What have you learnt from these activities?

2. What unfruitful evangelistic activities are you involved with? What needs to be done about this?

3. How, practically, can you improve the way your members are trained in personal evangelism?

4. Which of these forms of evangelism – friendship, street, social, celebration or caring – does your church use most? Which form does it use least? What steps can you take to ensure a balance between the different forms?

5. What fears most paralyse your evangelism? How should they be dealt with?

6. What steps should you take to make effective evangelism a higher priority in your church?

# God Gave Me A Dream

## Norman Barnes

### As told to
### Rod Boreham

CW00607398

## New Wine Press

# Contents

| | Page |
|---|---|
| Foreword | 5 |
| Introduction | 7 |
| **Chapter 1** | 11 |
| The World in My Heart | |
| Dreaming of Miracles | |
| Life Goes On | |
| Stepping Into A Dream | |
| **Chapter 2** | 35 |
| A Mother's Dream | |
| The World Begins in Goodmayes | |
| Split the Difference | |
| **Chapter 3** | 59 |
| Developing Links | |
| **Chapter 4** | 71 |
| More Than One Way To Have Children | |
| Adapt Or Adopt? | |
| What's In A Name? | |
| **Chapter 5** | 83 |
| Land of Dreams | |
| Land of Tears | |
| Fruit that will last | |
| **Chapter 6** | 107 |
| Awakening Dreams | |
| Tap, Tap, Tap | |
| Waltzing Around | |

# Chapter 7                                    119
India - Frustration and Fascination
Not For Shirts and Trousers
Orphans, Orphans and More Orphans
The Dream-Like Continent
Bazaar Experiences
Assassination
Men of Vision
Home At Last!

# Chapter 8                                    150
In Abraham's Footsteps

# Chapter 9                                    156
Go East Young Man!
Hong Kong
China
Thailand
Lessons To Be Learned

# Chapter 10                                   168
David's Tent
Stateside Again!

# Chapter 11                                   174
Still Dreaming After All These Years

# Foreword

A 'chance' engagement found me speaking at the local Pentecostal church's weekly youth meeting. The person booked to share had been taken ill and I was asked to stand in at the last moment. The handful of young people gathered gave me their eager attention and as I started to minister numbers suddenly doubled when a group of black christians piled in through the back door. My subject was 'Take the whole armour of God!' At the close I called for a fresh commitment to the service of Jesus and almost the whole meeting responded. I thought revival had broken out.

In the midst of all the prayer and shouts of praise was a young man weeping and crying out to the Lord for blessing as he dedicated himself to world mission. That young man was Norman Barnes and that meeting began almost thirty years of friendship and working together to date. It's not been without its hiccups, as you'll read, but I am profoundly grateful to Jesus that he caused our paths to cross and I believe the 'best is yet to come.'

In all those years Norman, and his lovely wife Grace, have not lost their hunger to see God move in power. They have never visibly wavered in their zeal to see precious people won to Jesus. Their concern for the needy world has only increased as they have travailed, ministered and journeyed to country after country. With the passage of time, to Norman's youth and enthusiasm, God has added faithfulness and wisdom and he has emerged as a modern pioneer and statesman in the cause of bridge-building and mission.

From the beach at Brighton to the more distant shores of Africa and Asia; from London's Soho to Hong Kong and beyond; from suburban mission hall to star-studded Texas, two words shine through in Norman's life, 'faith' and 'vision'. Without any ballyhoo or sentiment I'm proud to have Norman as my friend and know of no-one better to encourage you with tears and smiles to make your dreams come true.

JOHN NOBLE

# Introduction

11,000 young people attended Mission '87, a five day youth congress held in Utrecht, The Netherlands, and organised by T.E.M.A. (The European Missionary Alliance). Time and time again throughout the five days the challenge went out loud and clear to consider the call to evangelism and world mission. For many the Congress was a life altering experience as they surrendered to the call to serve God.

Day four was the one and only meeting for each national group. Around 600 people gathered for the British meeting. It was noisy in the hall, for behind the platform was a very flimsy partition, beyond which another meeting was taking place for a different national grouping. As Norman Barnes, Director of Links International and Vice Chairman of the T.E.M.A. national committee stood to speak, all he could hear behind him was the noise from the other meeting. He had no way of knowing just how much that noise could be heard by those attending the British meeting, or if the P.A. system he was about to use would be adequately powerful. The last thing he wanted was for people to be straining to hear what he had to say, or indeed go away from the meeting not having heard anything. Norman decided that there was only one thing to do to be absolutely sure about the whole matter. He had a message to give that he believed to be from God and so in order to overcome all the noise he simply stood at the microphone and attempted to shout over the top of the unavoidable din.

He poured out his heart to the young people listening intently to what he had to say. He told them how so many people get trapped by the concept of the will of God as a rigid, narrow, inflexible matter. Well meaning, enthusiastic and sincere people who are desirous of giving all they have and are in service to God, often are prevented from doing just that, because they are unsure whether it really is the will

7

of God for them to undertake some sort of service, whether at home or abroad. As a result many lives are wasted and the Kingdom of God suffers.

"Everyone of us" he said, "have been given dreams. We all have longings in our hearts to do something, to be something for God. The problem is, many of us do not realise that those dreams that we cherish have been put there by the Holy Spirit and he wants to see them become reality. Don't get all hung up about whether the thing you want to do is the will of God or not. Has God put a dream in your heart? What is it that you long to accomplish? Make your dream a reality. Tell someone about it, confess it to the Lord, pray about it and then look to God to open up the way for you."

At the close of his message, he asked people to gather in small groups and pray together about their dreams, asking God to establish them firmly in their lives. All around the hall hopes and aspirations began to be expressed, and not a few tears were shed as young people realised that the longings of their hearts were not merely fantasy and could actually become reality for them.

In the counselling room after the meeting there were a number of positive responses, with enquiries along the lines of what people could actually do about the dreams they held; a problem that any congress or mission is happy to have.

Each national grouping also had to fill in a response card for the whole event, and a number mentioned the fact that the national meeting where the speaker talked about dreams was the highlight for them.

There were one or two very negative responses to Norman's ministry. They mistook his shouting for raving and felt he had gone on an ego trip. Such is life for enthusiastic communicators!

Misunderstanding is nothing new to Norman. A man who dreams big dreams himself and works to see them fulfilled will inevitably be misunderstood. His enthusiasm will sometimes be regarded as being pushy and his determination

8

be mistaken for bigheadedness. His zeal may sometimes make people think he lacks sensitivity and his success will either cause admiration or jealousy. Norman has encountered all of these reactions, but still continues to dream and see his dreams fulfilled.

When he stood to speak at Mission '87, it was just one more fulfilment. An opportunity to share with young people about a few of the opportunities available to those who are prepared to go for the sake of the Gospel, and see many responding to the challenge was just one more desire that he had held in his heart.

This is the story of two dreamers, Norman and Grace Barnes, ordinary people from east London who dared to believe some of the incredible things God spoke to them about and who, through much joy, considerable sorrow and the miraculous and caring hand of their heavenly Father, have watched His purposes unfold for their lives, bringing blessing to themselves, and many, many others.

ROD BOREHAM

# Chapter 1
# The World in my Heart

People with a vision but no task may be labelled dreamers, but those who have a task and no vision will almost certainly live a life of boredom and drudgery. There is nothing more soul-destroying and frustrating than carrying out work for which there seems no real purpose; labour for which there would be little return in the way of personal fulfilment.

If I had to choose between the two groups, I know to which I would rather belong. I have always been a dreamer, always had hope in my heart that certain things would happen, and have done my best to pursue those dreams.

A dreamer is frowned upon in our culture. The term is usually associated with somebody who has got their head in the clouds; they are living in a world of unreality; always dreaming of what might be, rather than getting on with the here and now. And there may well be people like that, who only dream but never actually do anything about seeing their dreams become reality. Those who want their dreams to come true have certainly got to wake up!

Nothing of any significance has been achieved in the world without someone first dreaming of it happening. Whether it was an architect working on a revolutionary design for a building; a scientist seeking a cure for a killer disease; missionaries wanting to set up schools, hospitals and churches in some corner of the globe as yet unreached by the Gospel of Christ; or a married couple longing for a family. So many of the achievements and events in our lives start off as a seed thought that slowly fills our hearts and minds and becomes a vision worth pursuing, a goal to strive for.

Many of the noteworthy characters, people who made an

11

impression on the society in which they lived, would have been regarded as dreamers. The words of Martin Luther King ring loudly in my ears. "I have a dream" he declared to the thousands who gathered to hear him speak. Those words spoken so confidently, that inspired many, are etched with sadness now, when one remembers how dearly that great man paid for his dream. Knowing, however, that his life was on the line most of the time, did not stop him from pursuing his dream and taking practical steps to see it fulfilled.

Dreams, however, are not just for the 'great'. We all cherish hopes, desires and ambitions in our hearts which will be as diverse as we are. There are very few human beings who do not dream of achieving something in life, or improving themselves and their lot in some way. Some of those dreams could be very selfish and it might even be better if they were never fulfilled. On the other hand, more of our dreams than we care to imagine are placed in our hearts by a loving Father who wants His children to reach out, take hold of them and make them reality.

Almost from the moment I became a Christian at the age of 16 years old, God put a vision in my heart to reach the world. In retrospect, it must have seemed ludicrous to those who knew about my dream. Who did this young lad from Dagenham, Essex, think he was, believing that the Lord had spoken to him about touching and helping to meet some of the crying needs of our world? But believe, I did; even though I had no real conception of what this meant. All I knew was, I could not be content until I saw this dream fulfilled.

The youth group to which I belonged at Dagenham Elim Church was experiencing some extraordinary times of blessing. The Holy Spirit seemed to be doing a special work in the lives of the members of the group, which strangely did not seem to be touching the rest of the Church. On a number of occasions that we met the presence of God seemed to fill

12

the room in such a tangible way, that we found ourselves prostrated on the floor. The subject of being slain in the Spirit is a regular item for discussion in the current move of the Holy Spirit around the world, but in 1958 we simply referred to it as being flat on our faces before the Lord.

On one such occasion we met to seek the Lord. We were full of expectancy, young people with a burning desire to serve the Lord and know His power work in and through us. I was standing, praying, when the Holy Spirit touched me. My knees buckled and I found myself on my face before the Lord. For a period of about 2 hours all I could do was speak in tongues, but as I did this, I became aware of a vision so real, I felt that I could have reached out and touched it. The scene being portrayed before my eyes was so vivid, I felt as if I had been transported bodily out of the small meeting room to where this scene was taking place.

I could see myself on an elevated platform in a large building, preaching. As I spoke in tongues, so what I was saying seemed to correspond with what I heard myself preaching in the vision. I moved around on the platform, and looked out on a sea of black faces. I could see thousands of black people listening intently to what I had to say. As I preached, they responded eagerly to my words and at the close of the message I gave an appeal. Many came forward to the platform as a result to meet with God, and at that point the vision faded.

I was thrilled and deeply moved by what I had experienced. It took me some time to come back to reality. I knew somehow that what I had seen was a vision of a place in Africa and as I 'came round' I looked at the twenty or so other young people in the room. ''Have I been here all the time?'' I asked.

''Yes, of course you have,'' they assured me, slightly amused by the fact that I should even ask.

I explained what had happened to me. With the sort of confidence that only comes with youth I stated clearly, ''one

13

day God will get me to Africa.'' The look of incredulity on everyone's faces was enough to convince me that most of them were not as confident about the fact as I was. The leader of the meeting, Charles Calvert, had become a good friend to me and seemed to appreciate me. ''You believe it Norman,'' he said, ''and one day God will get you there.''

Those words were a great encouragement and gave me renewed enthusiasm and a trust in God to perform what he had shown me, even if no one else in the room believed me.

With hindsight I can see that it must have been difficult for them to accept what I was saying without any shadow of doubt. I was a bit of a loud-mouth and thought a lot of myself, and my statement must have sounded arrogant to say the least. But along with this less acceptable side of my nature, I did have a deep desire to serve God and was willing to undertake almost any task I was asked to do. Under the circumstances it might have been wiser to wait for a while before I shared with the rest of the group about the vision.

Joseph is one character in the Bible that I admire. Time and time again he literally bounced back from the pits, the depths of despair, eventually to rise to a position of immense power in Egypt and thus become the saviour of his family in a time of famine. But it required a lot of hard dealings by the Lord before his character was formed enough to cope with such an elevated position.

As a young man, he was his father's favourite. This undoubtedly caused jealousy amongst his brothers, and the gift of a rather expensive coat did nothing to endear him further to them. He also received dreams from time to time, and, whether out of naivety, youthful exuberance or wishing to be provocative is not clear, he wasted no time in sharing his dreams with his brothers. Which would have caused no problem, but for the nature of the dreams.

''I dreamt'' he announced one day, ''that we were binding sheaves of corn out in the field, when suddenly my sheaf rose and stood upright, while your sheaves gathered round

14

mine and bowed down to it. And I had another dream, and this time the sun and moon and eleven stars were bowing down to me.'' His family had no problem in interpreting the dreams and, needless to say, were less than overwhelmed by these proclamations. Hardly surprising and not very wise on Joseph's part. But I can identify with him. God had spoken to him quite clearly through the dreams, and before he had given any time to think about the repercussions, had blurted out the whole scenario. I feel sure, in spite of his brothers' reactions and all the subsequent events in his life, those dreams remained very real to him.

After the vision I received about Africa, I knew beyond all doubt that the dream God had put in my heart about reaching the world was going to be fulfilled. I felt confident that I would serve the Lord full-time and I would travel the world in the course of my ministry. The vision only served to confirm all those feelings, but like Joseph, I was sometimes insensitive as to when and how I shared these things. I cannot blame people for thinking that I was a big-head at the time.

Patience was also not very high on my list of virtues. I never doubted that God would perform what he had shown me, but I had one problem, I wanted him to do it immediately. I wrestled with him about it, plagued him, agonised over it, desperately wanting to see some action. The Lord was very gracious to me and spoke to me with these words, ''After you have received the promise, wait patiently.''

Joseph must have thought he had made it when he was appointed as chief servant in Potiphar's house. After the treachery by his brothers, he had good reason to believe that things were finally going to work out better. Maybe those dreams he had were closer to reality than ever, after all, he had a position of responsibility, and compared with his brothers, he was a man of some importance.

But we all know what happened. Refusing to have any-

15

thing to do with Potiphar's wife's advances and suggestions was the cause of another downfall. He had avoided sin and yet had been cast as the villain of the piece and put in jail. How excited he must have been when he was first given a job in Potiphar's house. How crestfallen he must have felt when his act of righteousness only seemed to take him a giant step backwards and down the social ladder, in fact to below the bottom rung. The questions must have plagued him. "How could this happen? I only did what was right. Why did God allow this?"

God used the situation to further his purposes for Joseph's life, develop the man's character and continue moulding him into the person he wanted him to be.

People who actively pursue their dreams and are impatient to see them come true, are prone to try and make things happen. Like Joseph, they find themselves making one or two false starts. Five years after I had received the vision about Africa, during which time the longing to see the vision fulfilled never left me, I thought the moment had come.

On a number of occasions I had been thrilled by films from the T.L. Osborn Evangelistic Association. They showed meetings held by the evangelist in different countries around the world, with vast crowds in attendance. Hundreds of people committed their lives to Christ and many miracles of healing were recorded. A film about such meetings in Ghana challenged and stirred me in particular. I could almost feel myself on the platform like T.L. Osborn, preaching to thousands of Africans. Imagine my excitement and sense of anticipation when an opportunity arose to meet the U.K. representative of the T.L. Osborn organisation. My mind ran riot! At last the door of opportunity was about to open. I was on my way to Africa!

I met the representative and told him of all my dreams and plans and how I was convinced God wanted me to go to Africa. I ws given an invitation to join the organisation, and my understanding was that this would eventually lead me to Africa. For the time being, however, they wanted me to travel around the U.K. showing films and generally promoting the work of the T.L. Osborn Evangelistic Association.

I left the meeting with the representative with hopes flying high. At last I felt something was really beginning to happen. Within a very short space of time, however, my enthusiasm began to dampen and a growing sense of unease about the whole proposal began to grip me. The question of financial support for the work I was to underake was unclear. I had also become engaged to Grace and I was unsure how this work would affect our relationship. These two factors, plus an overriding sense that I was actually pre-empting what God wanted to do, made me think again. Not long after, the proposals were dropped. God had put the world in my heart but he showed me that I would get to Africa in my own right. I was not to keep on trying to engineer the situation.

In spite of the fact that I knew this was right, I couldn't help feeling disappointed, but by this time I was involved in a ministry team called the 'Good News Team' as well as carrying out gainful employment in a Merchant Bank. I diverted all my energies into whatever opportunities for ministry came my way. Regularly, at weekends, the team would make its way to a designated place to preach in the open air. In summer, this would mostly take place at one of the coastal resorts, and we regularly preached to hundreds of people. It was nothing unusual to see members of the crowd weeping as we witnessed to them and it was a great thrill to lead many to a place of surrender to the Lord Jesus Christ.

## Dreaming of Miracles

While I was involved with the ministry team, another dream began to come to birth in my heart. Often, whilst travelling together I would sit with a man named Les Hilary. Whenever he broke bread he would say "thank you Lord for another week of perfect health". They were not just idle words, for he was a real testimony to divine health. I was greatly challenged by Les' attitude and began to seek God about the whole area of healing. I became aware of the importance of seeing the Gospel demonstrated in signs and wonders and not just preached. I began to see that the evangelistic ministry needed accompanying signs and miracles in order for people to know that God is indeed the Lord. I saw how important Jesus regarded the miracles that he did, not only in actually meeting people's needs, but in revealing who he was. It was through a miracle that the disciples first came to put their faith in him. After he had performed the famous, and for the host of the wedding reception, face-saving miracle of turning water into wine, we read the following words: *"This, the first of his miraculous signs Jesus performed in Cana of Galilee. He thus revealed his glory, and his disciples put their faith in him."* (John 2 v 11).

It began to dawn on the disciples who Jesus was after they saw this amazing manifestation of the power of God.

On another occasion, when Jesus was talking to the crowds, there were a number of religious leaders present displaying their usual cynicism and unbelief. Jesus was trying to explain who he was and how he was one with the Father. It seems to me that almost in frustration at the hardness of their hearts, he says *"Do not believe me unless I do what my Father does. But if I do it, even though you do not believe me, believe the miracles that you may learn and understand that the Father is in me, and I in the Father."*

I longed to see a manifestation of God's healing power in a way that would make people really sit up and take notice. I was grateful for the isolated incidents that we witnessed, but I knew that when I looked at the life of Jesus and the early Church, there was so much more of God's power available

18